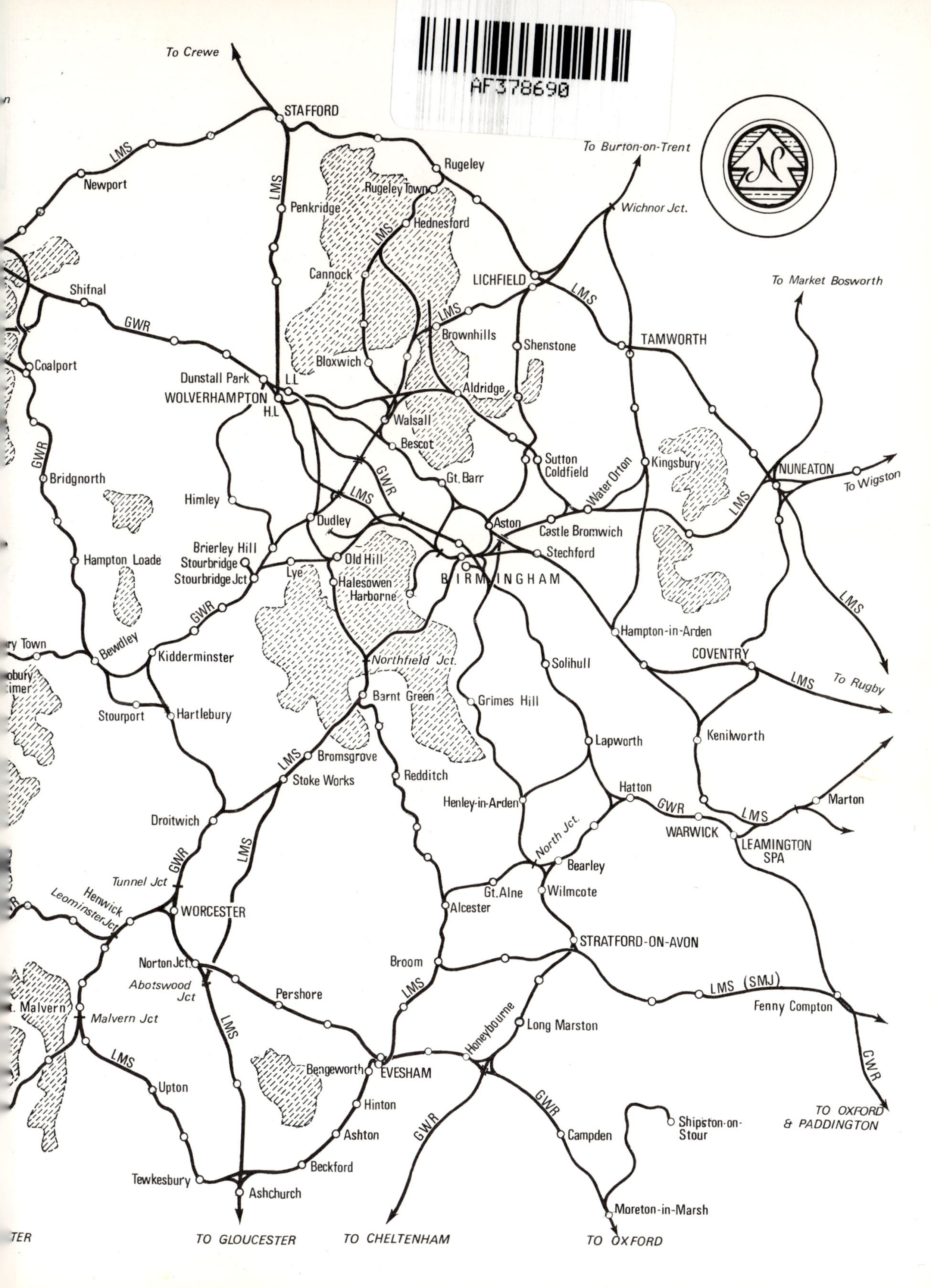
To Crewe
STAFFORD
To Burton-on-Trent
AF378690
Newport
LMS
LMS
Rugeley
Rugeley Town
Penkridge
Wichnor Jct.
Hednesford
LMS
To Market Bosworth
Cannock
LICHFIELD
LMS
Shifnal
GWR
LMS
Brownhills
Shenstone
TAMWORTH
Coalport
Bloxwich
Dunstall Park
L.L
Aldridge
WOLVERHAMPTON
H.L
Walsall
Bescot
Sutton
Coldfield
Kingsbury
NUNEATON
To Wigston
Bridgnorth
Himley
GWR
LMS
Gt. Barr
Water Orton
Dudley
Aston
Castle Bromwich
Hampton Loade
Brierley Hill
Stourbridge
Old Hill
Stechford
Lye
Halesowen
BIRMINGHAM
Stourbridge Jct
Harborne
GWR
Bewdley
Hampton-in-Arden
LMS
ry Town
Kidderminster
Northfield Jct.
Solihull
COVENTRY
To Rugby
obury
imer
Stourport
Hartlebury
Barnt Green
Grimes Hill
LMS
Kenilworth
Lapworth
LMS
To Oxford
Bromsgrove
Marton
Stoke Works
Redditch
Hatton
Droitwich
Henley-in-Arden
GWR
WARWICK
LMS
GWR
LMS
North Jct.
LEAMINGTON
SPA
Tunnel Jct
Bearley
Henwick
Gt. Alne
Wilmcote
Leominster Jct
WORCESTER
Alcester
STRATFORD-ON-AVON
Norton Jct.
Broom
Abotswood
Jct
Pershore
LMS
LMS (SMJ)
t. Malvern
Malvern Jct
LMS
Honeybourne
Long Marston
Fenny Compton
LMS
Bengeworth
EVESHAM
GWR
Upton
Hinton
Shipston-on-Stour
TO OXFORD
& PADDINGTON
Ashton
GWR
Campden
Tewkesbury
Beckford
Ashchurch
Moreton-in-Marsh
TER
TO GLOUCESTER
TO CHELTENHAM
TO OXFORD

West
Midlands
Branch Line
Album
BEWARE
TRAINS

West Midlands Branch Line Album

Anthony J. Lambert

LONDON
IAN ALLAN LTD

Acknowledgements

For their kind and valued assistance in
producing this book, I extend my appreciative
thanks to the following:

Messrs: Andrew D. Bannister, G. F.
Bannister, Harold D. Bowtell, Howard
Burrows, R. S. Carpenter, H. C. Casserley,
C. R. L. Coles, J. A. G. H. Coltas, G. Daniels,
E. J. Dew, T. J. Edgington, D. S. Fish,
C. Gammell, J. Spencer Gilks, E. T. Gill,
C. C. Green, R. C. N. Hanger, F. A. Haynes,
R. E. James-Robertson, M. Mensing,
David R. Morgan, Brian Morrison, Frank F.
Moss, J. A. Peden, L. W. Perkins, N. T. Pitts,
J. T. Rhead, F. W. Shuttleworth, J. N. Slinn,
D. Stagg, W. G. Sumner, E. W. Tennent,
J. E. Tennent, E. S. Tonks, A. Tyson, A. A.
Vickers, R. Vincent, P. B. Whitehouse, D. C.
Williams, T. E. Williams, E. Wilmshurst,
S. A. Wood.

Finally my particular thanks to Mr W. A.
Camwell for his constant and generous help.

Introduction

In common with most great historical or economic movements, the Industrial Revolution presents countless pitfalls for the writer who is invariably forced to generalise not only by limitations of space or breadth of subject but also the need to make sense of his subject. However, it does not seem too contestable to say that the entrepreneurs and engineers of the West Midlands provided most of the technical developments in the iron industry which made possible the Industrial Revolution.

Until the early 18th century, one of the main problems facing the iron industry was the growing scarcity of good quality timber, needed to produce charcoal for smelting. The Forest of Arden which filled the angle between the Severn and the Avon as far north as Wolverhampton, was being felled and the traditional centres of the industry in Sussex and the Forest of Dean were in decline. Abraham Darby freed the industry from its dependence on wood in 1709 by smelting iron with coal at his works at Coalbrookdale, set up on capital of a mere £3,500. It was left to his son and Henry Cort to develop iron production before full advantage of the discovery began to be taken in the 1780s, but his famous bridge across the Severn of 1779 anticipated the tremendous use that was to be made of cast iron during the next century. It was also at Coalbrookdale that the first cast iron cylinders for steam engines were made.

The problem of producing a stronger blast for furnaces and, much later, of powering

Left: The soft tranquility of rolling Warwickshire fields is captured in this view of No 6834 *Dummer Grange*, heading an early evening down freight just south of The Lakes Halt on 25 August 1962. In 1965 most goods trains over the North Warwickshire were diverted over other routes. / *M. Mensing*

Henry Cort's inventions of the puddling furnace and rolling mill were greatly helped by work being done in a Birmingham factory. In 1775, James Watt arrived in Birmingham to take advantage of the finest engineering skills then available in England at Boulton's workshops in Soho. Boulton's foreman was William Murdoch and it was he who inspired Watt to produce rotary motion from the steam engine in 1781. The ability to drive machinery from a steam engine was naturally one of the fundamental preconditions for large scale industrial production.

The first railway developments took place largely in the north of England although cast iron rails were used in Coalbrookdale in the 1760s and Trevithick's locomotive was tested there in 1802. However, Birmingham had reached industrial eminence and had become the centre of the canal system, largely completed by the 1770s, and it was only a matter of time before Birmingham figured in many railway proposals. It is commonly assumed that Birmingham, like Manchester, was a product of the industrial revolution but the village was mentioned in the Domesday Book and the first industries arose during the 16th century, largely concerned with iron. The de Bermingham family were succeeded as lords of the manor in the 16th century by the Dudleys and it was to connect Lord Dudley's colliery at Shut End with Ashwood Basin on the Staffordshire and Worcestershire Canal that the first railway in the area was opened in 1829. By 1883, the Dudley family had financial interests in ten collieries, three limestone works, an engineering yard and six ironworks so it is not surprising that Lord Dudley was able to build the line with his own men. The level section between two inclined planes was worked by a Stourbridge-built engine named *Agenoria* which now resides in the National Railway Museum.

The Shut End (or Pensnett) Railway was a mineral line only and it was not until 1838 that the first passengers left the town of Birmingham for Rugby in the first instance and later in the year, London. The acceptance of railways as an unmitigated blessing for mankind was not a common sentiment at the time. Sceptics could become quite hysterical in their epistolary warnings:

'...the solitary stranger, who had nobody to tell him better, would go swinging at the tail of the engine, bumping first on the iron-plates on this side, and then on the iron-plates on that side: and if he escaped being scalded to death by the bursting of his own engine, or having all his bones broken by the collision of another, he would be fain to rest for the night within some four bare walls, and gnaw a mouldy crust which he had brought in his pocket', etc, etc.

Fortunately for those responsible for raising capital to build the railways, there were sufficient men of vision in the land to subscribe the vast amounts of money necessary. In rural areas, construction of railways was tantamount to a public service by local benefactors as the prospects for a good return on capital were poor by comparison with those offered by other industries. In the West Midlands, the involvement of Lord Bateman (whose home was at Shobden Court) in the Leominster and Kington Railway may be cited as an example.

The benefits of railways in commerce and industry were quickly evident as easier and cheaper communications cut prices of consumer goods and raw materials. Towns and villages which were not served by a railway were naturally at a commercial disadvantage so that no community of any size readily resigned itself to being avoided by the rapidly spreading iron roads. Some railways were begun in the hope or expectation of becoming part of a through route, like the Bishop's Castle or the Potteries, Shrewsbury and North Wales Railway. Had these two fulfilled the destiny their promoters anticipated for them they would never have become the quaint concerns that have attracted historians and even national newspaper reporters of the twenties, always in search of novelty for their readers in the Northcliffe/Hearst 'circulation war'.

The region as a whole was well endowed with lines of character and charm. The fascination of the country railway has been expounded at length in books and magazines but one or two illustrations will not go amiss. The Great Western branches in Shropshire and Herefordshire depended as much upon the beauty of their surroundings for their attraction as on any innate qualities. With the Bishop's Castle and the Shropshire and Montgomeryshire Railways this was not the case. On the BCR, all the station clocks had stopped by 1933 and departure of the train at Bishop's Castle was prompted by the striking of the church clock. The staff at Bishop's Castle were not exactly hard pushed to perform their duties and on the occasions of a visit by Mr Roberts, the Receiver and Manager who worked in Wrexham, the driver would give three blasts on the whistle so that the staff could improvise bustling activity. In the late twenties, the staff at Bishop's Castle were disturbed to discover that a huge container which had arrived in a box van was obviously too large to be removed. It transpired that the porters at Craven Arms had had to remove part of the van's floor and had deliberately sealed it up to perplex the Bishop's Castle staff.*

In another 'Buggleskelly' situation, this time on the Shropshire and Montgomeryshire, a traveller in the early thirties presented himself at Llanymynech station at 8am and created some excitement by requesting a 1st class ticket. He was politely informed that although there were no 1st class carriages, they would be very pleased to let him have such a ticket!

Such eccentric concerns had no place in the harsher economic conditions facing the railways from the 1930s so that, over the decades, branch after branch closed at an accelerating pace until Arab politics forced a reappraisal of our railways' value. The outlook for their future is perhaps more hopeful than at any time since nationalisation and should remain so provided governments keep long-term objectives and considerations firmly in view rather than allow electoral expediency to influence their thinking. The positive

* Readers are recommended to Edward Griffith's entertaining account of the Bishop's Castle Railway.

approach by the West Midlands Passenger Transport Authority has done much to win back traffic to the railways.

But to most eyes, one looks in vain for charm in a modern railway. Three organisations in the West Midlands strive to preserve something to help our children understand a past that enjoyed a more leisurely pace and a sense of pride, a sadly deficient quality in our age. Each does it in a very different way. At Hednesford, in Staffordshire, a largely industrial collection of engines has been assembled in a Black Country setting while at Tyseley, the Birmingham Railway Museum is looking to the next century in its emphasis on preserving the machinery and skills that will enable our grandchildren to enjoy the sight of a steam engine at work. A considerable collection of engines and rolling stock has been built up and, with the valued assistance of Birmingham City Council, the Museum is planning to broaden its appeal by embracing educational sections of small exhibits and the history of the city's railways. Finally, the Severn Valley Railway, featured in this book in its pre- and post-preservation days, operates a service between Bridgnorth and Bewdley with a very large collection of locomotives and coaches. Several of the intermediate stations have been painstakingly restored with period fittings, hanging baskets and well-tended flower beds, and even the replacement of concrete sleepers by wood — commendable thoroughness which enhances the atmosphere of a journey on the line.

The inclusion of some lines in this book may occasion surprise. Certainly the promoters of the North Warwickshire and Oxford, Worcester and Wolverhampton Railways would have been chagrined at the description of their achievements as 'branch lines'. When opened several were not, but in recent years changes in investment policy have left many a main line a backwater or closed it altogether. The drawing of the boundaries is inevitably a subjective matter, determined by limitations of space and personal preference tempered by a concern to omit nothing of importance.

THE BEECHING
SPECIAL
4178

3626

Buildwas and Wellington

Left: The last train from Much Wenlock to Wellington on 21 June 1962 arrives at Doseley Halt behind Prairie tank No 4178. Opened in December 1932, Doseley Halt was one of four halts opened by the GWR in the 1930s between Buildwas and Wellington. / *M. Mensing*

Below left: Collett 0-6-0PT No 3626 between Ketley Junction and Ketley with the 5.50pm Wellington to Much Wenlock on 12 September 1959. This section was closed completely in 1962 but merry-go-round coal trains still run over the southern section to Ironbridge power station. / *M. Mensing*

Right: The 5.50pm for Much Wenlock makes a smokey exit from the bay platform at Wellington behind 0-6-0PT No 3732 on 6 August 1956. / *Brian Morrison*

Below: Wellington shed provided motive power for the branches to Market Drayton, Much Wenlock and, in later years, Coalport. On 22 July 1957, 2-6-2T No 4142 and 0-6-0PTs Nos 9630 and 5712 await their next duty. / *J. A. Peden*

Above left: In May 1957, the Saturdays only 12.48pm mixed from Ketley to Much Wenlock stands at Ketley behind 0-6-0PT No 3732. / *G. F. Bannister*

Centre left: Crossing at Coalbrookdale. No 4406 is about to leave with the 4.30pm Wellington to Much Wenlock on 15 July 1950. / *T. J. Edgington*

Below : The 3.05pm Wellington to Much Wenlock arrives at Ketley behind small-wheel Prairie No 4406 on 5 September 1947. The section from Ketley to Horsehay and Lightmoor Junction was briefly operated by the Coalbrookdale Iron Company, using its own engines, including some built at their works. / *W. A. Camwell*

Left: Just before steam ended on all West Midland workings, LMS 8F No 48220 finds the climb up Coalbrookdale hard work in her neglected condition. The empties are from Ironbridge Power Station. Green Bank Halt, in the foreground, was opened in March 1934 in an endeavour to stem the threat from bus competition. / *G. F. Bannister*

Below: A little known line ran from Hollinswood down sidings to Stirchley to serve a concentration of heavy industry. The 1¼ mile line was opened by the GWR in 1908 and closed in 1959. Pannier tank No 5745 is seen at Dark Lane ungated crossing in May 1956 with the thrice weekly working. / *G. F. Bannister*

Buildwas–Craven Arms

Above: Opened in stages during the 1860s, this line traversed some of England's most beautiful countryside. This view of Rushbury station in 1932 encapsulates much of the charm of the country station. / *L & GRP*

Left: Churchward 2-6-2T No 4400, built in 1904, shunts at Much Wenlock on 10 September 1949, two years before passenger services were withdrawn beyond Much Wenlock to Craven Arms. / *H. C. Casserley*

Above right: After withdrawal of passenger services beyond Much Wenlock, the section to Longville remained open for a daily goods working. Pannier tank No 9639 is seen at Longville on 25 July 1960. / *E. J. Dew*

Right: On 21 April 1951, 2-6-2T No 4401 enters Longville with a train for Craven Arms. The section between Craven Arms and Much Wenlock was operated by wooden staff while the section on to Buildwas was worked by electric train staff. / *W. A. Camwell*

LONGVILLE

LONGVILLE

Above: Collett 0-6-0PT No 9639 with a good head of steam passing Farley with a Much Wenlock train on 19 May 1962. / *J. Spencer Gilks*

Left: Small wheeled Prairie tank No 4401 runs into Farley Halt with an afternoon train to Craven Arms on 21 April 1951. / *W. A. Camwell*

Above right: The 8.16am from Wellington on 25 September 1954 arrives at Much Wenlock behind 0-6-0PT No 3732. The small signal box on the left dates from the opening of the line but was replaced by a larger structure almost opposite it. / *G. F. Bannister*

Right: Much Wenlock shed on 28 June 1926. Churchward's small-wheel 2-6-2T No 4401 is inside and sister engine No 4403 outside. Until the 1930s, Wolverhampton-built 0-6-0STs were the usual motive power although steam railmotor units were briefly tried from May 1906. The steep gradients proved too much for them. The shed closed on 31 December 1951 when passenger trains between Much Wenlock and Craven Arms were withdrawn. / *W. A. Camwell*

Wellington-Stafford

Above: Wellington station in the 1950s was a fascinating place to watch trains with so many branch trains to supplement those on the main line. On 27 August 1952, Fowler 2-6-4T No 42309 of Stafford shed leaves Wellington with 12.20pm Shrewsbury to Stafford. / *Brian Morrison*

Below: The frequent local service between Shrewsbury and Stafford ended in 1964 with the closure of the Stafford to Wellington section. Midland 2P 4-4-0 No 40461 leaves Wellington on 30 August 1952 with the 11.25am Shrewsbury to Stafford. / *Brian Morrison*

Right: The Shrewsbury to Stafford service provided plenty of variety. 'Patriot' No 45501 *St Dunstan's* passes Wellington Queen Street depot. / *Brian Morrison*

Below right: The Wellington to Stafford line was built by the Shropshire Union Railways and Canal Co and leased to the LNWR. Ivatt 2-6-0 No 46421 leaves Stafford with the 5.35pm for Wellington on 6 August 1956. Ten years later the line was closed completely from Stafford to Donnington. / *Brian Morrison*

BRITISH RAILWAYS
WELLINGTON QUEEN STREET
45501

46425

Above: On 15 July 1950, LNW 0-6-2T No 58904 waits to leave Newport, Shropshire, with the 5.45pm Newport to Wellington. A chartered town under a high steward until 1883, Newport was of sufficient importance to justify connection with the Severn by canal. / *T. J. Edgington*

Below: At Trench Crossing, a small shed was provided to house the engine which worked the Lilleshall Company sidings, serving Granville pit as well as the works. The sidings included some sharp curves so a short wheel base engine was desirable, although a pannier tank was assigned the job in 1949. On 29 September 1938, ex-L&Y 'Pug' No 11218 was being used. Class 5 No 5254 is passing the shed with a Stafford to Wellington train. The L&Y 'Pug' was soon to be replaced by one of the Caledonian type which was to remain at Trench until 1947 when the shed was closed and the engine transferred to Wellington. / *W. A. Camwell*

Wellington–Nantwich

Below: The prime use of the Great Western route to Crewe from Wellington was for through good trains. No 5919 *Worsley Hall* nears Adderley station with a northbound fitted freight on 12 August 1961. / *M. Mensing*

Bottom: No 4943 *Marrington Hall* calls at Hodnet station with the 12.15pm Wellington to Crewe local on 15 April 1963. The Great Western ran such a sparse train service over the line that they were happy to allow the North Staffordshire Railway to operate a train from Market Drayton to Hodnet on market days.

Above: Until May 1956, trains ran from Stoke-on-Trent to Market Drayton and here Fowler 2-6-4T No 42360 is about to run round its train before returning to the Potteries. 2-6-2T No 5109 stands in the main platform with a Crewe to Wellington local. The date is 8 November 1952.
/ *Harold D. Bowtell*

Right: The signalman of Wellington No 4 box watches GW 2-6-0 No 6368 thread its way on to the main line with a freight from Crewe on 4 July 1959. The line closed to passengers in 1963 and to freight in 1967. / *M. Mensing*

Below: The North Staffordshire shed at Market Drayton.
/ *Real Photographs*

Below right: Fowler 2-6-4T No 42376 stands at the island platform at Market Drayton with a train for Stoke while a GW 2-6-2T calls with a Wellington-Crewe local on 6 August 1949.
/ *W. A. Camwell*

WELLINGTON No 4
6968

42376

Coalport LNW

Above: Part of the Coalport branch was converted by the LNWR from the Shropshire Canal along which traffic from the china works, moved to Stoke in 1926, had once travelled. The line was opened from the junction at Hadley to Coalport in 1861. LNW Coal Tank No 58904 waits to leave the terminus with the 2.35pm to Wellington on 15 July 1950. / *T. J. Edgington*

Centre right: Passenger services were withdrawn in 1952 but goods traffic to Coalport continued until 1960 and to Stirchley until 1964. On 23 April 1955, the Stephenson Locomotive Society and Manchester Locomotive Society ran a special train over Shropshire branches. It is seen here at Coalport with Dean Goods No 2516. / *Harold D. Bowtell*

Below right: The last Webb 2-4-2T to be built, No 6757 in 1897, waits to leave Coalport in 1949. The first coach is an LNW rebuild of two former 6-wheelers. Passing loops on the branch were provided at Oakengates and Dawley. / *W. A. Camwell*

Severn Valley

Above: Great things were confidently expected of the Severn Valley Railway by its promoters. Running powers were to be exercised over the Chester and Holyhead and the Mayor of Bridgnorth was 'sanguine that no more remunerative line would be found in the Kingdom'. Such myopic hopes proved illusory and help was needed from the Oxford, Worcester and Wolverhampton Railway to open the line in 1862. A Fowler 2-6-4T leaves the junction of Buildwas for Shrewsbury in the spring of 1957. / *G. F. Bannister*

Below: Passenger services between Shrewsbury and Bewdley were withdrawn in September 1963. Pannier tank No 3788 calls at Bridgnorth with the 1.45pm from Shrewsbury on 18 August 1962. / *E. Wilmshurst*

A southbound goods headed by 2-6-2T No 4114 takes water at
Bridgnorth on 30 August 1962. / *M. Mensing*

Above: Beside the Severn, 2-6-2T No 4129 passes Hoards Park
golf course just north of Bridgnorth with a coal train on
30 August 1962. / *M. Mensing*

Passenger traffic was not heavy in later years except on
bank holiday weekends when the line would become a hive of
activity with excursions from towns in the West Midlands. It was
sometimes difficult to find space for engines on Kidderminster
shed. Railcar W32 was sufficient for the 2.5pm Kidderminster to
Shrewsbury on 14 June 1960, seen here calling at Hampton
Loade. / *E. J. Dew*

Above: The Tenbury and Bridgnorth lines met some distance outside Bewdley but no physical connection was made until the station was reached. Standard 2-6-2T No 82004 approaches Bewdley with the 1.45pm Shrewsbury to Hartlebury on 20 June 1959. / *M. Mensing*

Centre left: The sidings in this view of Bewdley are now happily full of preserved rolling stock and a splendid cast-iron loo again adorns the island platform. 2-6-2T No 4175 enters with the 2pm Hartlebury to Shrewsbury on 2 March 1957. / *E. J. Dew*

Below left: Stanier 2-6-2T No 40110 arrives at Ironbridge and Broseley with the 1.45pm from Shrewsbury on 27 February 1960. / *E. J. Dew*

Shropshire and Montgomeryshire

Above: The convoluted history of the Shropshire and Montgomeryshire Railway is all that one would expect of a line which came under the aegis of Col H. F. Stephens. For 31 years, between 1880 and 1911, it provided the peculiar sight of a derelict railway, as strange then as an abandoned and overgrown motorway would be now. The largest station on the Railway was Kinnerley Junction where the engine shed was situated. This view, taken in the 1930s, is looking west with the Criggion branch on the left and the line to Llanymynech straight ahead. / *Loco Publishing Co*

Below: At Llanymynech, the S&M met the Cambrian line from Oswestry to Welshpool and a Manchester Locomotive Society special train is seen here at the branch platform on 22 May 1955. The coaches are from the Ealing-Southend (via District Railway and LTSR) service. / *Harold D. Bowtell*

Right: During the war the S&M was taken over by the War Department and remained under a dual military/Western Region administration until closure in 1960. In 1954 the section from Shrewsbury to Llanymynech was relaid and this photograph of the MLS special at Maesbrook suggests that preparations were in hand to relay the remainder. / *Harold D. Bowtell*

Below right: Gazelle was built as a 2-2-2WT by Dodman of King's Lynn for William Burkitt, twice Mayor of Lynn. The engine was stabled at Lynn and used on business trips over the M&GN and on one occasion as far afield as Chesterfield. Seating for four was provided at the back of the cab. In 1911 it was purchased by Col Stephens who had it converted to an 0-4-2WT by Bagnall. *Gazelle* is now in the National Railway Museum. / *W. A. Camwell*

Left: Kinnerley shed in May 1936. The two engines are the Ilfracombe goods *Hesperus* and LNW 0-6-0 No 8182. The two LNW coal engines were normally employed on stone trains from the quarries at Criggion to Meole Brace exchange sidings, situated on the Shrewsbury and Welshpool Joint line. / *W. A. Camwell*

Centre left: In 1932, the S&M bought two of Webb's small-wheeled 0-6-0 coal engines, Nos 8108 and 8182. The latter is seen here at the S&M platforms at Llanymynech on 28 May 1932. / *H. C. Casserley*

Below: Shrawardine station in c1909. The diamond-shaped signal was turned to face trains if a stop was required. The 'Way In' notice seems somewhat superfluous. / *G. M. Perkins*

Right: On 26 June 1955, the Birmingham Locomotive Club ran a special train over the S&M. It is seen here waiting to leave Shrewsbury Abbey behind WD 0-6-0ST No 193. / *T. J. Edgington*

Below right: Former London and South Western Railway Ilfracombe goods 0-6-0, named *Hesperus* by the S&M waits to leave Shrewsbury Abbey c1913. Eight years after the line was closed in 1880 by the Board of Trade for being unsafe, the engines were auctioned, fetching between £85 and £305 apiece. Col Stephens purchased engines from the London, Brighton and South Coast Railway as well as the LSWR to resuscitate the line in 1911. / *G. M. Perkins*

WAY IN

SHRAWARDINE

Minsterley and Snailbeach

Above: Passenger services over the former GW and LNW Joint line to Minsterley were withdrawn in 1951 but a healthy goods traffic in dairy products, coal and cattle feed continued until official discouragement drove the traffic on to the road. This view is taken almost from the dead end at Minsterley on 23 January 1965. / *Harold D. Bowtell*

Below: A joint Stephenson and Manchester Locomotive Societies tour was run over the line on 11 September 1965 and Ivatt 2-6-0 No 46512 is seen here passing the 3- lever ground frame at Minsterley. / *Harold D. Bowtell*

Snailbeach District Railway

Left: This 3¾ mile line was opened in 1877 to 2ft 4in gauge primarily to transport lead from the mines in the Snailbeach area which had been worked since the Roman occupation. These were abandoned c1900 but the line remained open to carry stone which by the 1940s was confined to the Shropshire County Council quarry at Callow Hill. On 11 June 1943, Kerr Stuart 0-4-2T No 2 built in 1901, leaves Pontesbury for Callow Hill. / *L. W. Perkins*

Below: The steam engines were withdrawn in 1946 due to the condition of the boilers and gravity working down the 1 in 37 commenced. One of the two ex-ROD Baldwin 4-6-0Ts, No 3 and No 2 stand outside Snailbeach shed on 21 April 1950. They were cut up later that year. / *G. F. Bannister*

Top: Snailbeach shed c1925 with Kerr Stuart No 2 and Baldwin No 4. On the right are the remains of Bagnall 0-6-0ST delivered new to the line in 1907. It was intended for a rebuild soon after Col Stephens took over the railway in 1923, but it was never carried out. / *LPC*

Above: Snailbeach station in the 1920s looking towards Pontesbury. The company is still in existence and as a reminder of Col Stephens' involvement, the head office is in Tonbridge. / *LPC*

Right: Baldwin No 3 commenced work at Snailbeach in January 1923 after a rebuild at Bagnalls in 1918, necessitated by its condition following war service in France. / *W. A. Camwell*

Bishop's Castle Railway

Above: The Bishop's Castle Railway was an even more impecunious affair than the S&M, being in Chancery for most of its existence and never enjoying the assets of the longer system. The Railway's largest engine was *Carlisle*, an 0-6-0 built by Kitson in 1868 and purchased by the BCR from a Carlisle contractor in 1895. *Carlisle* is seen here at Bishop's Castle on 30 May 1932. / *H. C. Casserley*

Below: The promoters intended building a line from Craven Arms to Montgomery on the Cambrian with a branch to Bishop's Castle and the BCR were still trying to persuade the GWR to help realise this object as late as 1924. The section beyond Lydham Heath was never built, occasioning reversal of all trains there. *Carlisle* is about to leave Lydham Heath along the barely discernible track on 30 May 1932. / *H. C. Casserley*

Left: Carlisle on a mixed train approaching what is thought to be Eaton station. Coaching stock consisted of second-hand acquisitions from the LSWR, LNWR, Brecon and Merthyr and a third hand purchase from the Neath and Brecon.
/ C. C. Green Collection

Below: No time was wasted in dismantling the BCR after closure. *Carlisle* is seen here on the demolition train on 9 May 1936, less than a month after the end of services. By the end of February 1937, lifting was completed and *Carlisle* cut up.
/ W. A. Camwell

Bottom: After closure, what was left of the stock was concentrated at Plowden so that demolition of the Bishop's Castle end could begin. BCR No 1, formerly GWR 0-4-2T No 567, was cut up at Plowden where she is seen here on 14 May 1936. */ W. A. Camwell*

Above: The modest but spruce station at Lydham Heath. Two mixed trains each way with an additional trip on Mondays, Fridays and Saturdays was the usual service. / *G. M. Perkins*

Centre right: Stretford Bridge Junction at Craven Arms with the BCR on the left and the Shrewsbury and Hereford Joint line on the right. Stretford Bridge Halt may be seen beyond the signal box which was abolished as a block post and dismantled following closure and lifting of the BCR. The S&H charged £200pa for BCR running powers into Craven Arms. / *G. M. Perkins*

Right: Two of the BCR's 19 goods vehicles are seen here at Plowden on 9 May 1936. / *W. A. Camwell*

Woofferton–Bewdley

Above: The western section of the line between Woofferton and Tenbury Wells was partly operated as a separate entity and before the grouping was in joint ownership by the GWR and LNWR. On 10 June 1957, Collett 0-6-0PT No 4641 shunts the stock for the 7.50pm to Kidderminster into the platform at Woofferton. / *M. Mensing*

Below: The centenary of passenger services between Woofferton and Tenbury was missed by one day, lasting from 1 August 1861 to 31 July 1961. The driver of W7 surrenders the staff to the signalman at Woofferton on 27 March 1957. The shed at Woofferton was situated just behind the railcar. Clee Hill may be seen in the distance. / *E. J. Dew*

Above right: Although the station at Easton Court is near the hamlet of Little Hereford, it was named after what was probably a nearby country house although no trace of it remains. On 24 April 1961, 0-4-2T No 1445 leaves for Woofferton. The distant signal is for Little Hereford Crossing, from where the ground frame at the Birmingham Railway Museum originated. / *E. T. Gill*

Right: Pannier tank No 3601 enters Tenbury Wells from Bewdley while 0-4-2T No 1445 waits to leave with the 7.55am to Woofferton on 24 April 1961. The signal box was of unusual design with steeply pitched roof and stone lintels. A factory now covers the site. / *E. T. Gill*

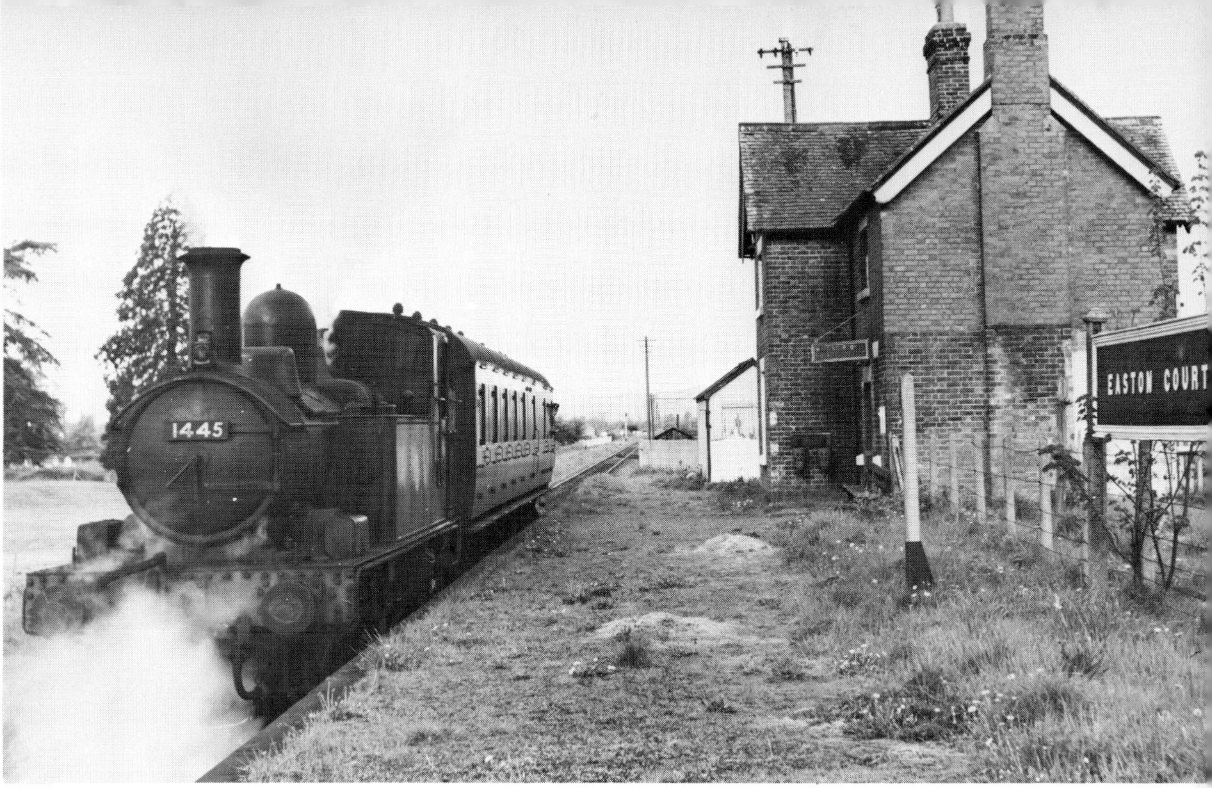
1445
EASTON COURT

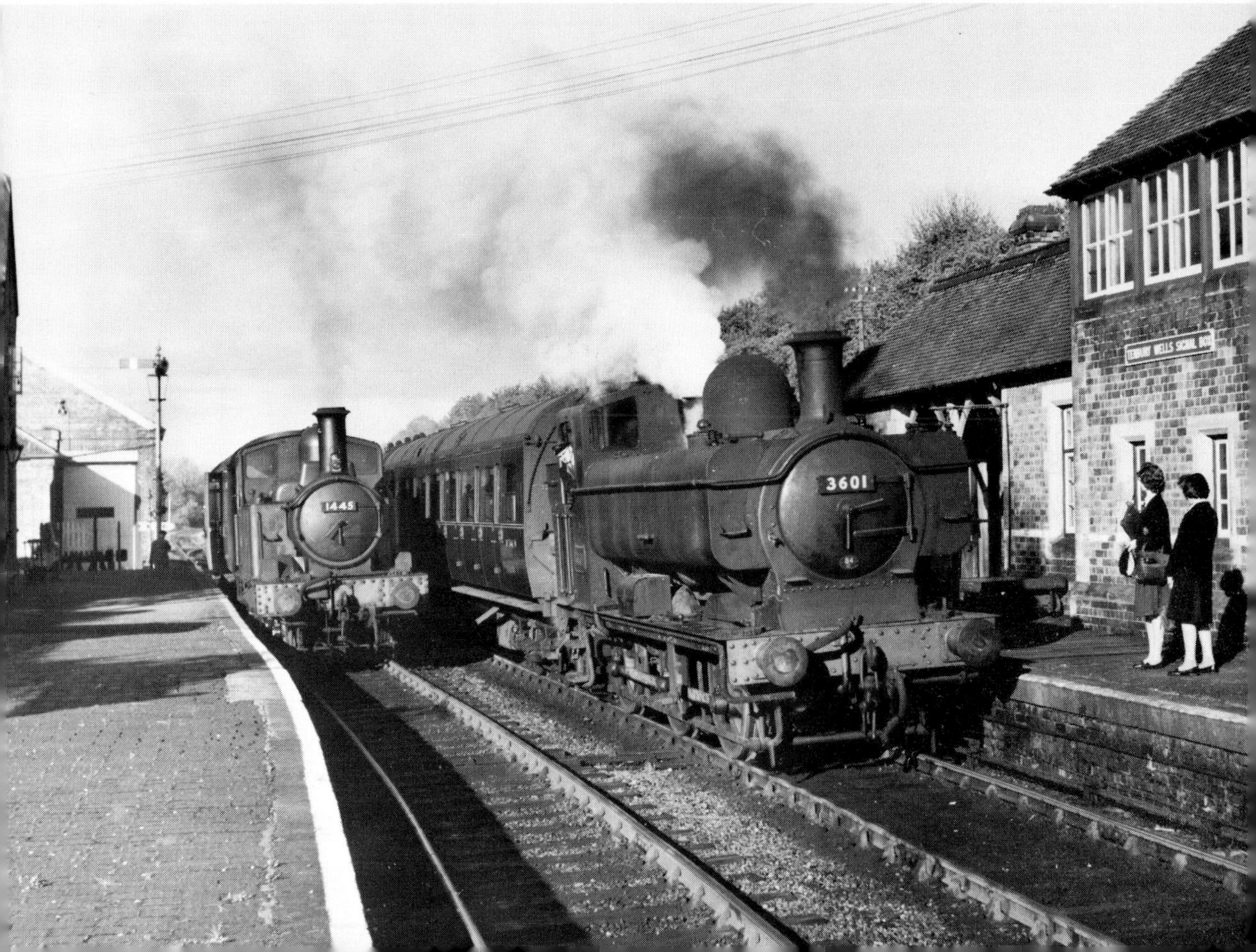
1445
3601

BURY MORTIMER

Pannier tank No 3601 has its tanks replenished at Cleobury Mortimer on its way to Bewdley on 24 April 1961. / *E. T. Gill*

Right: Between Cleobury Mortimer and Bewdley the line passes through Wyre Forest. Prairie tank No 4175 is pictured amidst the forest with the 2.18pm Bewdley to Tenbury on 29 July 1961. / *E. J. Dew*

Below: GW 0-6-0PT No 3619 calls at Neen Sollars with the 4.10pm Kidderminster to Tenbury on 27 July 1962. Note the milk churns. / *W. G. Sumner*

Bottom: Just before reaching Bewdley, the line crossed the Severn at a point near the entry of Dowles Brook. Railcar W22 is seen crossing the brick and lattice girder bridge with the 1.45pm Worcester to Tenbury on 18 March 1861. / *E. J. Dew*

CM and DPR

Below: The Cleobury Mortimer and Ditton Priors Railway was intended to facilitate the opening up of mineral deposits on Lord Boyne's estate, especially the valuable Dhu stone which was expected to contribute over 80% of gross receipts on the railway. The line was opened in 1908 with two Manning Wardle saddle tanks. *Burwarton*, GW No 29, is seen here at Ditton Priors on 30 March 1938. / *R. S. Carpenter Collection*

Bottom: During the war a number of ammunition dumps and a depot were created along the tranquil CM & DP, far from any obvious target for German bombers. The Admiralty took over the line in 1939 and again on 1 May 1957 until closure in 1965. An Admiralty freight waits to leave Cleobury Town for Ditton Priors on 14 April 1960 behind a Ruston 0-4-0 diesel. / *E. J. Dew*

Stourport

Right: Collett 0-6-0PT No 4613 leaves Stourport on Severn with the 4.10pm Hartlebury to Bewdley on 9 April 1958. Bank Holiday excursion trains had to pull up twice, blocking the level crossing for five or ten minutes. / *E. J. Dew*

Below: 'Crab' No 42897 passes Foley Park Hall on 16 August 1955 with a special from Burton-on-Trent and Walsall to Bewdley and Stourport. The sidings on the right serve the British Sugar Corporation plant which during the war was also used by Smethwick Drop Forgings. / *W. A. Camwell*

Clee Hill

Above: The mineral only line to Titterstone Granite quarries and Clee Hill was opened in 1864 and vested in the Shrewsbury and Hereford Joint in 1893. Y3 Sentinel No 68164 was at Clee Hill shed for less than a year, arriving from Wrexham in November 1956 and being replaced by former Swansea Harbour Trust 0-4-0ST No 1142 in autumn 1957. No 68164 is seen conveying chippings from the quarries to the head of the incline down to Bitterley on 27 March 1957. / *E. J. Dew*

Below: The sidings at Clee Hill were worked by a small engine stabled there and a Ludlow engine worked the section to the foot of the cable incline at Bitterley. On 15 August 1958 Hudswell Clarke 0-4-0ST No 1142, built in 1911, shunts at Clee Hill. / *Brian Morrison*

Top: The cable worked incline was powered by a stationary steam engine at the summit. Empty and loaded wagons are seen here passing at a turnout on 27 March 1957. / *E. J. Dew*

Above: A small signal box controlled the sidings at Bitterley and provided communication with the engine house at the top. This view was taken in April 1955. / *T. J. Edgington*

Left: Pannier tank No 8701 has stalled on the 1 in 20 approaching Bitterley yard in the summer of 1956. Goods traffic to Bitterley and Middleton ended in December 1962. / *G. F. Bannister*

Below and bottom: Two views of Ludlow shed on 28 June 1936 with Webb 2-4-2T No 6738 outside. Inside the shed are Metropolitan 2-4-0T No 3562, formerly at Southall shed and not withdrawn until 1949, 2-6-2T No 4527 and 0-6-0PT No 9714. In 1925, a LNW 0-8-0 and a GW small wheeled 2-6-2T worked the line to Bitterley. Until 1893 Clee Hill line was an independent concern and owned one 0-6-0ST. The wagons are owned by the British Quarrying Company. / *W. A. Camwell*

Top: The top of the incline at Clee Hill on 3 April 1955 showing the common centre rail. The incline closed in November 1960. / *T. J. Edgington*

Above: LMS Sentinel No 7164 at Clee Hill shed on 13 May 1937. Before the grouping, a LNW Ramsbottom 0-4-0T was the usual shunter at Clee Hill. / *W. A. Camwell*

Left: A former ROD saddle tank built by Baldwin in 1916 (works number 43201) was bought by the Clee Hill Quarry Co and worked at the summit until being scrapped c1939. / *F. E. Hemming*

Kington

Above left: Of the immediate towns and villages served by the branches radiating from Titley Junction, Kington was the most important with its thriving woollen mills and Richard Meredith's early iron foundry. The railway had reached the town in 1820 with a 3ft 6in tramway from Eardisley on the Brecon to Hay tramway. In July 1954, 0-4-2T No 1445 waits to leave Titley for Leominster with a train from Kington. Note the indicator on the home signal. / *E. J. Dew*

Centre left: When the line to New Radnor was built, a new station at Kington was constructed enabling the old station, to the left but out of view in this picture, to become the goods depot. Pannier tank No 7416 takes water at Kington on 11 April 1956 before working a goods over the Presteigne branch. / *G. F. Bannister*

Below: The Leominster and Kington Railway opened in 1857. Passenger services did not quite survive the century, being withdrawn in 1955, but the SLS marked the opening with a centenary tour on 27 July 1957. The train is seen here arriving at Kington behind 0-4-2T No 1455. / *G. Daniels*

Presteigne

Below: The branch to the Radnorshire county town of Presteigne opened in 1875. Trains ran to Kington rather than Titley Junction where the branch met the Leominster to New Radnor line. The passenger service was withdrawn during the 1951 winter coal shortage and never resumed. Pannier tank No 7437 is seen here at the terminus with the daily freight on 27 August 1960. / *E. J. Dew*

Bottom: The SLS Leominster-Kington Centenary special at Presteigne on 27 July 1957 with 0-4-2T No 1455. Until the withdrawal of passenger services, motive power was provided by Kington shed which usually accommodated two engines with three crews until closure on 5 February 1951. / *G. F. Bannister*

Hereford Hay and Brecon

Above: Opened in stages from 1862 to 1864, the Hereford to Brecon line was to become the Midland's route to South Wales although their efforts to tap some of the lucrative traffic in the area were never as successful as the other interloper, the LNWR. Through trains were cut back from 1931 when the Swansea to Hereford passengers ceased running and by BR days the route was seldom used as a goods artery. The last important working was the train of ICI liquid ammonia tanks from Dowlais Central to Haverton Hill (Durham). The train is seen here passing the former Brecon and Merthyr shed at Talybout-on-Usk on 27 May 1959 behind 0-6-0PTs Nos 8727 and 8780. / *D. S. Fish*

Below: Hay station was one of the rare cases where the station was in a different county to the town it served, the station being in Herefordshire and the town in Brecknockshire. Standard 2-6-0 No 78004 arrives at Hay with a freight from Hereford on 17 February 1962. / *E. T. Gill*

Right: Until 1941, Hay was the northern destination of trains on the Golden Valley line from Pontrilas. The section from Dorstone to Hay was dismantled as a wartime economy. Ivatt 2-6-0 No 46509 leaves Hay with the 12.42 Hereford to Brecon on 23 April 1962. / *G. Daniels*

Below: The lines which radiated from Three Cocks Junction to Moat Lane, Brecon and Hereford were all closed to passengers on 31 December 1962, marked by an SLS railtour over the lines on the previous day. Ivatt 2-6-0 No 46511 leaves Eardisley for Hereford on 9 January 1961 while a sister engine shunts in the goods yard. / *E. T. Gill*

Below right: Soon after nationalisation, a Midland 3F passes Dean Goods No 2556 with a Hereford bound goods at Moorhampton. / *P. B. Whitehouse*

MOORHAMPTON
NO ADMITTANCE
2556

Above: On 18 August 1959, the signalman at Eardisley Junction exchanges Webb and Thompson staffs with the driver of 0-6-0 No 2230 as it leaves for Hereford. The junction for Titley was behind the engine. / *J. Spencer Gilks*

Below: On 21 June 1951, L&Y 0-6-0 No 52414 leaves Hereford with the 9.20am for Brecon. The signalbox on the right is Worcester Sidings while just beyond Newtown Road overbridge is Barton and Brecon Curve box. The Worcester Sidings to Moorfields Junction curve and the Barton and Brecon curve were both opened in February 1893 when Midland trains ran to Barr's Court station instead of Barton. / *W. A. Camwell*

Leominster–Worcester

Below: It took 36 years from authorisation to complete this 24 mile line. Three separate companies were involved and were equally impecunious. Bromyard was the most important intermediate town as this busy scene on 11 May 1952 indicates. A pair of Dean Goods on goods workings are seen from a Leominster bound train headed by an 0-4-2T. / *H. C. Casserley*

Bottom: On 15 September 1952, all traffic between Leominster and Bromyard ceased, the section becoming a store for over 600 old and private owners' wagons, mostly from the Swansea area. Pannier tank No 4614 runs round its train on 23 June 1961. / *R. E. James-Robertson*

Above: The last train from Bromyard to Leominster before lifting of the track commenced was a Stephenson Locomotive Society special run on 26 April 1958 with small-wheeled Prairie No 4571 as motive power. */E. T. Gill*

Left: Pannier No 8793 enters Leigh Court with the 5.45pm Worcester to Bromyard on 17 April 1964. The line was controlled by electric train staff and Leigh Court was the only staff station without a loop. */E. J. Dew*

Golden Valley

Above: Opened in stages during the 1880s and closed in 1897/8, the Golden Valley Railway was bought by the Great Western in 1899 and re-opened in May 1901 after being brought up to acceptable standards. The track was flat-bottomed and the line never justified more than one engine in steam working. The date when this view of Dorstone was taken is not recorded. / *L & GRP*

Below: The goods to Dorstone waits to leave from the bay at Pontrilas behind 0-4-2T No 5818. / *W. A. Camwell*

Above: No 5818 at Dorstone on 21 June 1951. The GWR gradually replaced the flat bottom track but no signalling was provided. Goods traffic was cut back to Abbeydore in 1953.
/ *W. A. Camwell*

Centre left: Brass-domed 0-4-2T No 1437 stands in the bay at Pontrilas with the Golden Valley branch train. The 18¾ mile journey to Hay took 80 minutes. In 1941, the line beyond Dorstone was closed completely and passenger services over the whole line ceased.
/ *G. M. Perkins*

Below left: Pontrilas shed with 0-4-2T No 1437 taking water c1909. The shed was still open in 1938, housing 0-4-2T No 5818.
/ *G. M. Perkins*

Ashchurch–Malvern

Below: Although the Midland Railway ceased to exist almost 40 years before this photograph was taken, its artefacts predominate. Midland Class 3 No 43754 stands at Ashchurch with the 5.12pm for Upton-on-Severn on 26 April 1961. / *R. E. James-Robertson*

Bottom: The short section from Ashchurch to Tewkesbury was opened as early as 1840, but 24 years were to elapse before trains could run to Malvern. On 23 August 1958, Stanier 0-4-4T No 41900 stands at Tewkesbury. / *G. Daniels*

Above: Tewkesbury shed with Midland Johnson 0-4-4T No 58051 and 3F 0-6-0 No 43754 which later worked the last train to Tewkesbury and Upton. The shed survived the withdrawal of passenger services to Tewkesbury in August 1961 and two engines remained there, one for the twice-daily goods to Upton and the other for the Redditch line. / *Author's Collection*

Right: During the worst excesses of British Rail's Dark Age in architectural policy, much of E. W. Elmslie's beautiful station at Great Malvern was demolished. Fortunately the cast iron pillars with their ornate capitals which support the canopy survive and the enterprising local engineer held a competition at the art school for repainting them. LMS 2-6-2T No 40116 is seen at the station on 9 September 1949 before services from Upton were withdrawn in 1952. / *H. C. Casserley*

Below: Stanier's ten 0-4-4Ts were the last engines to be built with that wheel arrangement. No 41900 waits to leave Upton with the 1.30pm to Ashchurch on 23 August 1958. In September 1960, this engine was briefly tried on Much Wenlock to Wellington trains. / *E. Wilmshurst*

Below right: Johnson 0-4-4T No 1338 stands at Upton-on-Severn on 26 August 1947. Note the ornate diaper patterns and barge-boarding on the station building. / *W. A. Camwell*

GREAT
MALVERN
CLOAK ROOM
GREAT WESTERN
PARCELS OFFICE
TELEGRAPH
OFFICE

UPTON-ON-SEVERN
1338

Above: Midland 0-4-4Ts survived for over 10 years after nationalisation on the Tewkesbury line. No 58051 is seen here at Ripple with the usual single coach in 1952. / *W. A. Camwell*

Below: The designation 'level crossing' rarely refers to the crossing of two separate railway lines. Through running between Malvern and Evesham was made possible by this crossing at the north end of Ashchurch station. The southbound express is headed by Class 5 No 45460. / *W. A. Camwell*

Barnt Green-Ashchurch

Below: Perhaps the busiest secondary route in the West Midlands, the Barnt Green to Ashchurch line provided a useful diversionary route to the Midland main line over the Lickey Hills as well as generating considerable local traffic. On 23 April 1960, Ivatt 2-6-0 No 43013 leaves Alvechurch for New Street. / *M. Mensing*

Bottom: The shed at Redditch was situated near the North signal box and coal yards and was the home of up to six engines before dieselisation. In the 1930s, four of Deeley's 0-6-4Ts were shedded there until replaced by 2-6-2Ts. After the war Fowler 2-6-4Ts and Ivatt 2-6-0s predominated. This view of Fowler 2-6-4T No 42334 and a Midland Class 3 0-6-0 was taken in 1954. / *Photomatic*

Above: The line to Redditch is still open pending improvement under the enlightened administration of the West Midlands Passenger Transport Authority. Fowler 2-6-4T No 42383 calls at Redditch with the 8.10am New Street to Evesham train on Sunday, 30 March 1958. / *M. Mensing*

Left: It is seldom that a passenger service has to be withdrawn because of the poor condition of the track but this was the reason for withdrawing trains between Redditch and Evesham. Ivatt 2-6-0 No 46492 leaves Redditch with 1.12pm New Street to Evesham on the last day, 29 September 1962, after which a substitute bus service conveyed passengers to Evesham. / *M. Mensing*

Above right: Ivatt 2-6-0 No 43047 leaves Studley and Astwood Bank in March 1962. The first section of the line was opened in 1859 between Barnt Green and Redditch but it was another nine years before trains could run through to Ashchurch. / *F. A. Haynes*

Right: LMS 2-6-2T No 171 waits to leave the isolated junction station at Broom on 8 September 1949. Even then, passengers could no longer change for Stratford-upon-Avon, services having been withdrawn in 1947. / *H. C. Casserley*

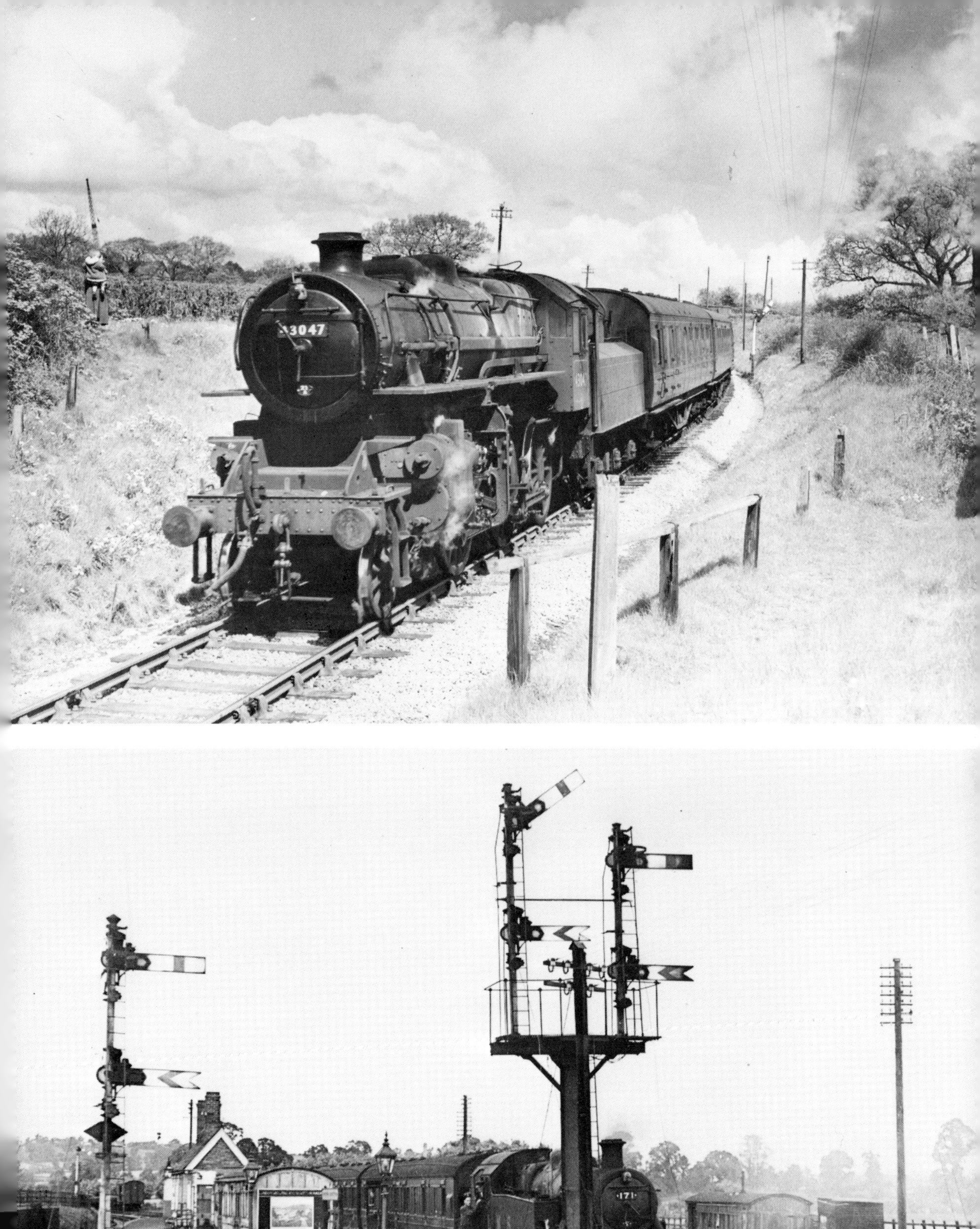

Below: The juxtaposition of the Great Western and Midland stations at Evesham may be clearly seen in this view of Ivatt 2-6-0 No 43046 backing on to its train after running round on 14 April 1962. / *M. Mensing*

Right: Broom North Junction on 11 June 1962 with Ivatt 2-6-0 No 43033 approaching on a northbound train. The south curve at Broom was not put in until 1942 so until then Midland trains for Avonmouth Docks had had to reverse at what became the north junction. / *J. Spencer Gilks*

Bottom right: Ivatt 2-6-0 No 43012 is watched by a young admirer as it enters Hinton station in March 1962 on its way to Ashchurch. The section from Evesham to Ashchurch was closed to passengers in June 1963 and to goods in September of that year. / *F. A. Haynes*

Above: Fowler 2-6-4T No 42416 of Saltley shed enters Ashton-under-Hill station with the 12.24pm Evesham to Ashchurch in 1962. / *F. A. Haynes*

Below: Unusual motive power for an Evesham to Ashchurch local. Collett 0-6-0PT No 3745 calls at Beckford on 15 June 1963. It was the last train to call at the station. / *M. Mensing*

Above: On 26 August 1947, Johnson 0-4-4T No 1338 passes Bengeworth with an Evesham to Ashchurch goods. The engine was withdrawn later that year. / *W. A. Camwell*

Below: Beckford under snow. The single coach of the 12.27pm Evesham to Ashchurch pauses there in January 1963. / *G. Daniels*

Stourbridge Town

Above left: The short branch from Stourbridge Junction to Town station was opened in 1879 and by 1915 there were 55 trains daily to Town and 60 to Stourbridge Junction. 0-4-2Ts were the usual motive power and No 1414 is seen here at Stourbridge Town on 10 September 1949. / *H. C. Casserley*

Left: Steam and diesel railcars worked the branch until 1958 when multiple units took over. The line is still open but the once busy goods extension to Stourbridge Basin closed in 1965. W14W waits to leave Town station on 19 October 1957. / *Harold D. Bowtell*

Above: Collett 0-4-2T No 1438 and autocoach leave Stourbridge Town for the Junction on 1 May 1957. In the following year, multiple units took over and No 1438 was sent to Southall. / *T. J. Edgington*

Right: In later years, the goods branch to Stourbridge Basin was operated as a separate entity from the passenger line, no physical connection being made. The arrangement may be seen in this view of pannier tank No 9624 passing Town station in July 1962. / *E. W. Tennent*

North Warwickshire

Above: The initially independent Birmingham and North Warwickshire Railway might have had Pollitt and Robinson 4-4-0s running over it rather than Bulldogs had the MSL/Great Central not run into financial difficulties and come to an agreement with the Great Western to improve its London approaches. But it opened under the auspices of Paddington in 1907/8 and was to prove an invaluable through route to the West Country and South Wales. A relief up 'Cornishman' is seen climbing Wilmcote bank behind No 7019 *Fowey Castle* on 15 June 1957. / *M. Mensing*

Below: It took 33 years from authorisation to construct and open the 3½ mile branch from Rowington Junction to Henley-in-Arden. The independent concern was taken over by the GWR in 1900, eight years before the new Henley station on the North Warwickshire line was opened, relegating the old station to a goods depot. Local trains from Lapworth to the new Henley station ran until 1915. This view of the old station when still a terminus was taken c1900. / *G. M. Perkins*

Above right: GW 2-6-0 No 6387 comes off the Bearley line with a southbound goods on 23 September 1957. The line between Bearley and Hatton was not doubled until 1938/9, entailing the construction of a new station at Claverdon. / *M. Mensing*

Right: The 4.30pm Moor Street to Henley-in-Arden leaves Grimes Hill behind 2-6-2T No 5104 on 28 May 1957. Moor Street was opened in 1908 to cope with the extra trains following construction of the North Warwickshire line and development of suburban services. / *T. J. Edgington*

Shipston-on-Stour

Above: The branch to Shipston was originally part of the horse-drawn 4ft-gauge Stratford to Moreton Tramway. In 1853 it was converted to standard gauge by the Oxford, Worcester and Wolverhampton Railway and later adapted by the GWR for steam working. On 24 April 1955, Deans Goods No 2474 enters Shipston with a Railway Enthusiasts Club special. */ T. E. Williams*

Above right: The branch to Stratford left the Shipston line at Longdon Road. It was last used in about 1900 but its course is still easily discernible and may be seen beyond the crossing gates on the right. Longdon Road station closed in 1929 when the passenger service ended. This view showing the delightful countryside through which the line passed was taken in October 1958. */ M. Mensing*

Right: The shed at Shipston was closed in 1917 when the train service was reduced from four to two daily. Thereafter engines were provided by Worcester or Kingham sheds. Standard 2-6-0 No 78008 waits to leave Shipston on 3 June 1960, just before closure to goods. */ G. Daniels*

BRIERLEY HILL
9733

Stourbridge Junction-Priestfield

Left: The Oxford, Worcester and Wolverhampton Railway opened between Stourbridge and Priestfield in stages between 1852 and 1854. Pannier No 9733 trundles a short southbound freight through Brierley Hill on 26 August 1961. / *M. Mensing*

Below left: Prairie 2-6-2T No 4104 leaves Brierley Hill with the 5.35pm Snow Hill to Dudley and Brettell Lane on 26 August 1961. / *M. Mensing*

Above: On 28 April 1962, 4-6-0 No 7817 *Garsington Manor* leaves Dudley with the 4.10pm Kidderminster to Snow Hill, having set back out of the platform and restarted to gain the LNW line as far as Horsleyfield Junction. The line from Stourbridge to Dudley is still open for the freightliner depot and goods traffic. / *E. J. Dew*

Below: The 11.7am Stourbridge Junction to Wolverhampton train nears Prince's End behind 0-6-0PT No 9674 on Sunday 30 July 1961. The local service between these towns was withdrawn exactly a year later. / *M. Mensing*

Right: GW 0-6-0PT No 3677 passes Bilston West with the 3.57pm Wolverhampton to Kidderminster on 28 April 1962. / *E. J. Dew*

Below: Prairie tank No 5151 leaves Priestfield with the 5.27pm Stourbridge Junction to Wolverhampton on 30 April 1960. Priestfield continued to be served by locals from Wolverhampton to Snow Hill until they were finally withdrawn on 6 March 1972. / *M. Mensing*

Below right: No 6828 *Trellech Grange* takes the Oxford, Worcester and Wolverhampton line at Priestfield with the 4.48pm Wolverhampton to Worcester on 1 June 1957. / *T. J. Edgington*

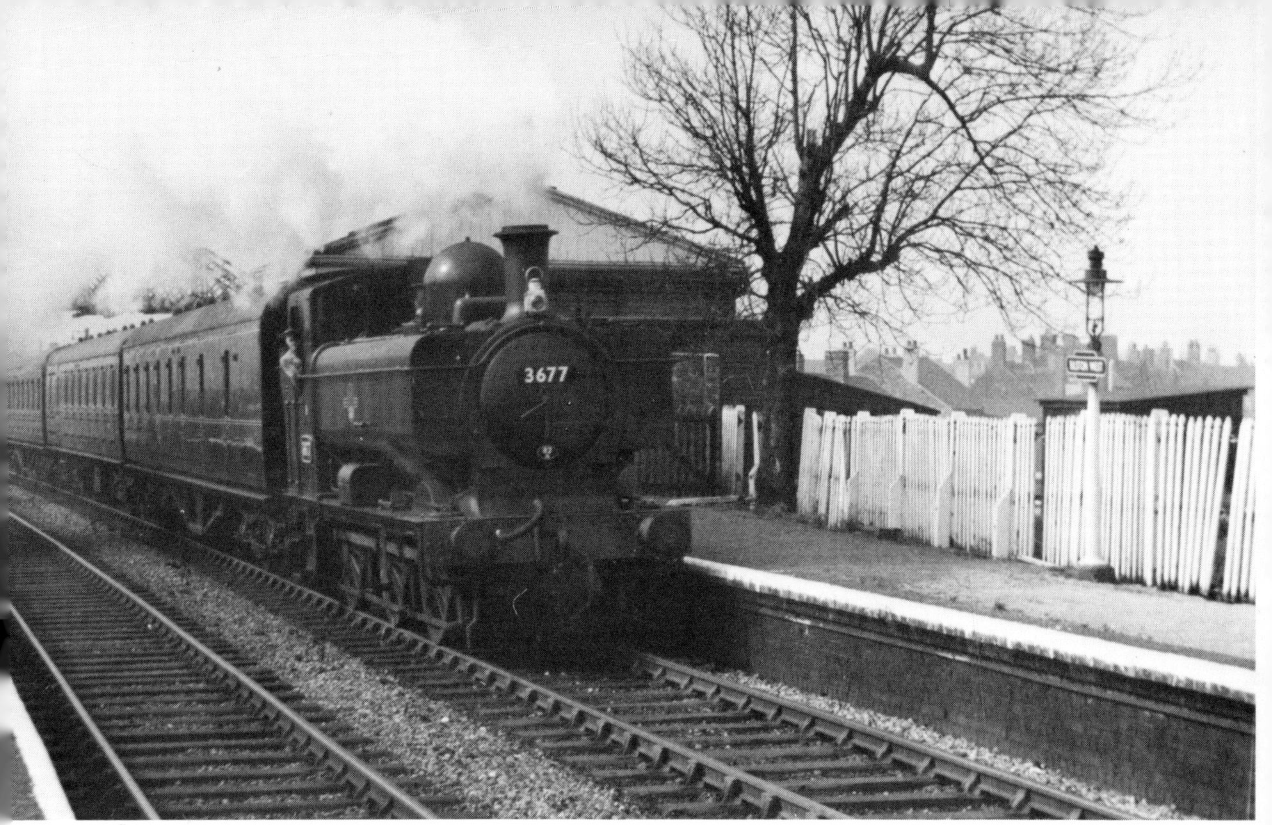

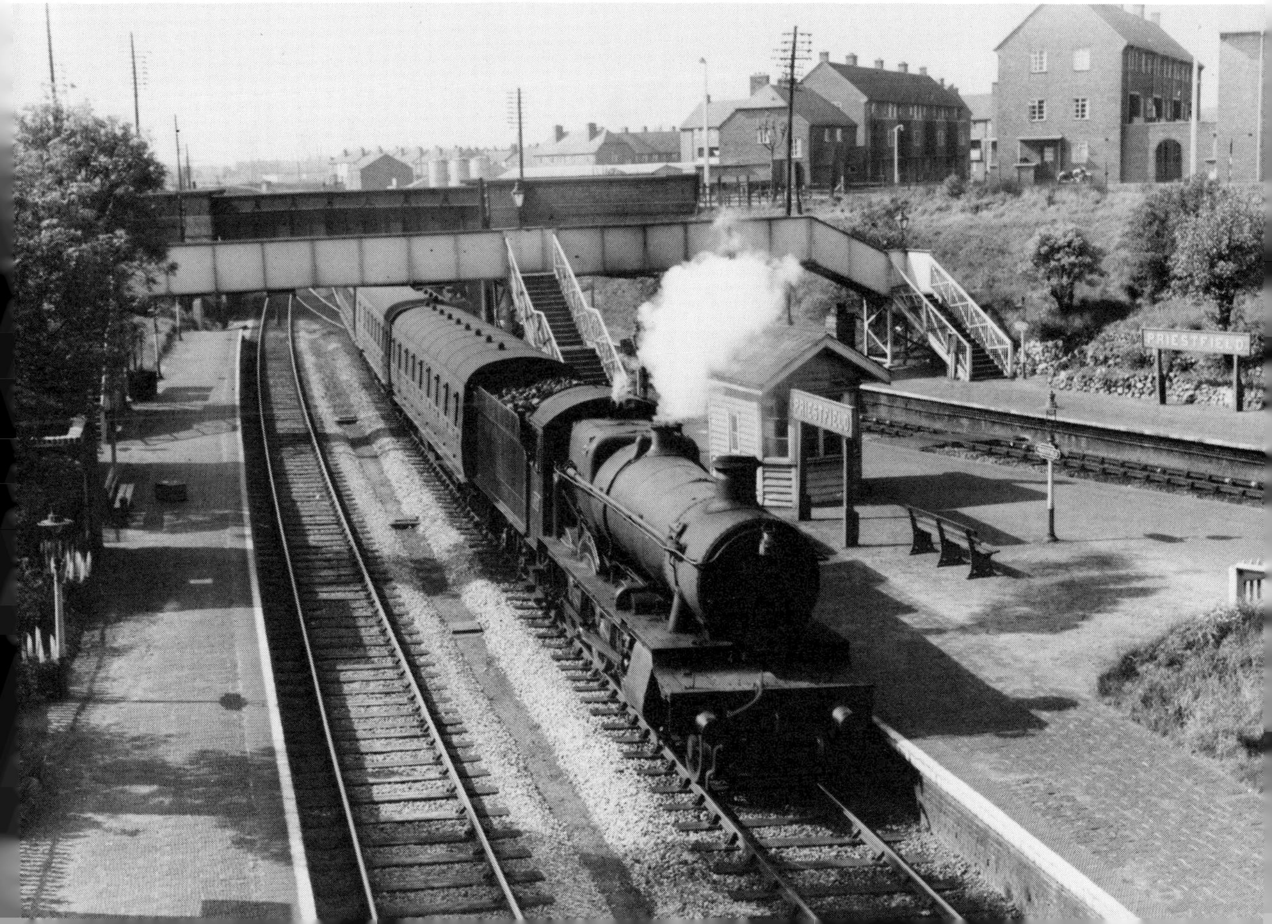

PRIESTFIELD
PRIESTFIELD

Branches to Old Hill

Above left: Ordinary passenger services between Old Hill and Halesowen ceased in 1927 but workmen's trains continued until 1958. Pannier tank No 7435 takes water at Old Hill with a Longbridge train. / *P. B. Whitehouse*

Left: In a typical Black Country landscape, 2-6-2T No 4111 takes the Windmill End line at Blowers Green (Dudley and Netherton until 1921) with a diverted Wolverhampton to Snow Hill local on 23 September 1956. Engineering works were being carried out near Priestfield. / *M. Mensing*

Above: The first siding and platform for the Austin works at Longbridge were installed in 1915 and the sidings are still open. A SLS railtour on 30 May 1959 calls at the station behind Johnson 2F No 58271. / *E. J. Dew*

Below: On 20 August 1957, 0-6-0PT No 7449 croses the lattice viaduct over Twiland Wood with the 6.55pm Longbridge to Halesowen goods. The viaduct was demolished in 1965. / *T. J. Edgington*

HALESOWEN JUNCTION
S.L.S.
SPECIAL
58271

Left: The Austin works on the 1926 Ordnance Survey map is a tiny square surrounded by green fields. By the time the SLS operated a tour over the line on 30 May 1959, it had grown somewhat but rail traffic is not as heavy as it could be, perhaps because of the vested interest in lorry production. Midland 2F 0-6-0 No 58271 passes Halesowen Junction box at Longbridge. / *T. J. Edgington*

Below left: A half-cab 0-6-0PT on an Old Hill to Longbridge workmen's train. / *W. Leslie Good*

Above: With numerous coal mines in the area, the stations on the Old Hill to Dudley line were prone to subsidence. Windmill End was reconstructed in concrete soon after this view of 0-6-0PT No 6422 and autocoach was taken. / *W. A. Camwell*

Below: Railcar W8 calls at Darby End with the 5.01pm Old Hill to Dudley on 28 May 1956. / *T. J. Edgington*

Dudley Port and Dudley

Above left: Stanier 0-4-4T No 41902 calls at Great Bridge North on 30 June 1955 with the 6.48pm Walsall to Dudley. Services between these two points were withdrawn in 1964. / *W. A. Camwell*

Centre left: On 24 April 1949, main line trains normally using the Stour Valley line were diverted via Walsall. Special trains were run to provide a connection at Walsall and one is seen here at Dudley Port behind 2-6-2T No 41225. / *W. A. Camwell*

Below: Pigeon baskets await loading at Great Bridge North on 12 May 1950 as LNW 2-4-2T No 46712 calls with the 1.42pm Walsall to Dudley. Note the locomotive boiler on the bogie bolster. / *T. J. Edgington*

Left: The Dudley to Walsall line was part of the former South Staffordshire Railway, opened in 1849 to comply with their Act but in 1850 for normal traffic. A shuttle service operated between Dudley and Dudley Port for the Stour Valley line. In 1915, a service of 60 trains made the four minute journey on weekdays and 17 on Sundays. On 24 August 1950, No 46712 of Walsall shed waits to leave Dudley Port for Dudley. / *P. B. Whitehouse*

Below: In 1866, the Great Western built a 1½ mile spur from Swan Village to the South Staffordshire line at Horsley Fields Junction, providing one intermediate station at Great Bridge South. Running powers were enjoyed over the LNW to Dudley. The 5.08pm Dudley to Snow Hill enters Great Bridge South behind 2-6-2T No 5185 on 20 August 1957. / *T. J. Edgington*

Soho Line

Above: In September 1949, Stanier 2-6-0 No M2951 passes Handsworth Junction, now named Perry Barr West Junction, with a Stetchford to Wolverhampton goods. The short link between Soho and Perry Barr opened in 1888 and proved a useful means of relieving congestion at several points by virtue of its double facing junctions at each end. The clump of trees in the distance is Barr Beacon.
/ *W. A. Camwell*

Right: About 10 years later, Class 5 No 45189 passes Handsworth Junction with an empty stock train.
/ *W. A. Camwell*

Harborne

Above left: The LNW branch to Harborne was an early victim of buses and an awkward junction with the main line which somtimes occasioned intolerable delays, the odd passenger getting off the train, walking up the embankment and catching a bus to the city centre. It closed to passengers in November 1934 but not until 1963 for goods. The last Webb 2-4-2T to be built, BR No 46757, has just traversed the Harborne branch with an SLS special on 3 June 1950 and is seen on the crossover at Monument Lane. / *Frank F. Moss*

Centre left: Immediately after Harborne Junction, the branch veered west and crossed the Birmingham Canal Navigation. This view was taken on 2 November 1963. Usual motive power for the line was Webb 0-6-2Ts and 2-4-2Ts with occasional visits by a Jumbo 2-4-0 in the early days and Fowler 2-6-2Ts just before closure to passengers. / *T. J. Edgington*

Below: Unusually the Harborne Railway remained independent until the grouping, refusing three offers of purchase by the LNWR who worked the line. In 1914 there were 27 trains each way. No 46757 descends the 1 in 66 to Harborne with the same special. / *Colourviews Picture Library*

Stanier 2-6-2T No 40080 enters Sutton Coldfield on 27 July 1955 with the 6.26pm Lichfield to New Street. The line is still open for freight, retaining a double facing junction at Castle Bromwich. / *T. J. Edgington*

Castle Bromwich to Wolverhampton

Above left: If time was of no consequence and the traveller desired the sight of fields between Birmingham and Wolverhampton, the only route to choose was the Midland which ran a circuitous service from New Street via Sutton Coldfield and Walsall until 1965. The sincerity of Victorian environmentalists may be judged by their appeasement with the promise of cheaper coal following an outcry against the idea of a railway bisecting Sutton Park! Stanier 4-6-0 No 45333 restarts an empty return excursion on 4 August 1957, the occasion of the Boy Scout Jubilee Jamboree in Sutton Park. The station is Streetly. / *M. Mensing*

Left: Fowler 2-6-4T No 42327 enters Sutton Park with the 5.40pm New Street to Walsall as Stanier 2-6-4T No 42429 prepares to leave with the 5.17pm Wolverhampton to New Street. As early as 1909, Midland trains were diverted on to the LNW route between Walsall and Wolverhampton, obviating the need for reversal at Walsall. / *T. J. Edgington*

Above: Until 1929, Aldridge was the junction for passenger trains to Brownhills. Here Stanier 2-6-4T No 42601 enters Aldridge with the 1.45pm Walsall-New Street on 8 October 1955. / *W. A. Camwell*

Below: On 5 June 1949, Stanier 2-6-4T No 42604 waits to leave Sutton Park with the 4.30pm train to Walsall. / *T. J. Edgington*

Above: The SLS toured Black Country lines on 26 May 1951 and the unusual formation is seen here at Aldridge with 2-6-2T No 41226. / *T. J. Edgington*

Below: Passenger services between Walsall and Wolverhampton via the Midland line were not withdrawn until 1931 although through trains from New Street had been diverted via the LNW since 1901. A Fowler 2-6-2T runs through Wednesfield station with a diverted train. / *W. A. Camwell*

Rugeley to Walsall

Above: One of the major problems when this line was opened in 1859 was theft. It was discovered that the engine crew would stop the train in a desolate spot on Cannock Chase, rifle the most promising van with the guard's help and conceal the loot in a purpose-built cave. Stanier 4-6-0 No 44926 climbs through Hednesford station with a diverted New Street to Manchester train on 17 June 1962. / *M. Mensing*

Below: A Rugeley to Walsall local leaves Bloxwich station behind Stanier 2-6-4T No 42562. Midland 0-4-4 and 0-6-4 tanks were common on the line in the 1920s. / *W. A. Camwell*

S.L.S
SPECIAL

WAY OUT
43858

Oxley to Brettell Lane

Left: The raison d'etre of this line was the opening of several new collieries on the Earl of Dudley's estate at Baggeridge near Himley. Opened in May 1925, it was single track except for the southern 2¾ miles which utilised the old Kingswinford mineral branch after doubling and relaying. A triangular junction was provided at Oxley. A SLS special passes the southern point of the triangle at Oxley Branch Junction Signal box. / *W. A. Camwell*

Below left: In January 1956, 4F 0-6-0 No 43851 passes Himley with a Crewe to Worcester freight. Near Himley, the line passes close to Holbeach House where the Gunpowder Plot conspirators made their last stand and were captured. The line closed completely in 1965. / *G. F. Bannister*

Below: Although local passenger services were withdrawn as early as 1932, the line was a useful route for excursion traffic, avoiding the busy Wolverhampton to Snow Hill section. In August 1960, Class 4 4-6-0 No 75006 leaves Oxley Branch Junction with empty stock of the 9.32am Bournemouth Central to Wolverhampton Low Level en route to Romsey via Wombourne and Stourbridge Junction. / *G. F. Bannister*

Kenilworth

Left: Webb 2-4-2T No 6754 calls at Kenilworth with a train for Coventry in 1938. Passenger services between Leamington and Nuneaton were withdrawn in 1965 but from 1977, expresses from Paddington and Oxford have used the line to serve the National Exhibition Centre. / *Locofotos (J. A. G. H. Coltas)*

Below left: Coventry railcar No 3 leaves Kenilworth for Coventry in 1937. These were the first pneumatic tyred railcars built entirely in this country. The first trial was on the Rugby-Wansford section and 75mph was reached. The cab was positioned on one side to give a clear view of ground signals. / *Locofotos (J. A. G. H. Coltas)*

Below: Johnson Class 2 0-6-0 No 3704 calls at Kenilworth with a Leamington train on 28 August 1936. The Coventry to Leamington workings were one of the last preserves of Webb 2-4-2 tanks, two still being shedded at Warwick in late 1952. / *Locofotos (J. A. G. H. Coltas)*

Bottom: Ivatt 2-6-2T No 41322 enters Kenilworth on 16 August 1958 with the 1.20pm Nuneaton to Leamington. Warwick shed closed with the dieselisation of these workings on 17 November 1958. The five engines, an 8F and four tank engines, were sent to the GW shed at Leamington. / *Brian Morrison*

LNW to Leamington

Above: Perhaps because of its position as an eminently fashionable town where society partook of its healing waters, Leamington Spa's genteel traffic was assiduously sought by the railway. The Great Western even ran a train to Malvern via Worcester from 1861 so that a tour of watering places could be encouraged. The LNW ran to Leamington only over branch lines but important ones. In 1938, eight coaches were required for this working to Nuneaton behind Webb 0-6-2T No 6890 and 'Cauliflower' 0-6-0 No 8430, seen here near Kenilworth. / *Locofotos (J. A. G. H. Coltas)*

Below: Kenilworth Junction with Webb 2-4-2T No 6660 on a local to Leamington. On the left is the line to Berkswell opened in 1884. In the same year, the doubling of the line between Kenilworth Junction and Milverton was completed. / *Locofotos (J. A. G. H. Coltas)*

Right: The LNW could never decide what to call their stations at Milverton and Leamington. What was to become Warwick (Milverton) bore nine names in 110 years and Leamington Spa Avenue six in 100 years. The difficulty lay in the conflict between the ancient county town and the upstart but respectable neighbour. Three years after the last change of name, Stanier 2-6-2T No 40078 waits to leave Leamington Spa (Avenue) for Coventry on 17 July 1954. / *Brian Morrison*

Below right: The importance of the LMS route to Leamington may be judged by the allocation to Warwick shed in 1928 of three 'Experiments' and three 'Precursors'. On 8 May 1958, Fowler 2-6-4T No 42345 leaves Leamington Spa (Avenue) with the 5.17pm to Coventry and Nuneaton. / *M. Mensing*

Right: The last train to call at Birdingbury station arrives behind Ivatt 2-6-2T No 41227 on 13 June 1959, the last day of services between Rugby and Leamington. One wonders what has induced such patriotic sentiments in the lady on the right when the state is depriving her of what even Wordsworth would probably concede was civilised transport in comparison with the alternatives. / *M. Mensing*

Below: Webb 2-4-2T No 46683 calls at Marton with a Rugby to Leamington train. At one time both the Rugby and Weedon lines had a through coach from Euston to Leamington. The Weedon coach was a brief affair but the service via Rugby ran until 1932. / *W. A. Camwell*

Below right: Built by Armstrong-Siddeley Motors Ltd, these railcars were powered by a V12 engine, delivering 280bhp at 3,200rpm, and achieved five miles per gallon. No 2 was photographed at Leamington Spa (Avenue) station in 1937. / *Locofotos (J. A. G. H. Coltas)*

Special Trains

Above left: On 21 May 1955 the Stephenson Locomotive Society ran a special over the Cleobury Mortimer and Ditton Priors Railway. Dean '2021' pannier tank No 2144 with spark arresting chimney at Cleobury North. / *Harold D. Bowtell*

Above: The train was taken back to Birmingham by Dean Goods No 2516 which is seen here leaving Cleobury Mortimer. / *Harold D. Bowtell*

Left: When 4-4-0 No 3440 *City of Truro* passed through Dunstall Park station on 30 March 1957 with the Festiniog Railway Society's annual special, it seemed inconceivable that the adjacent works would be closed within seven years. The station itself closed on 4 March 1968. / *G. F. Bannister*

Above: In June 1955, the Birmingham Locomotive Club toured the Shropshire and Montgomeryshire behind WD 0-6-0ST No 193 which is now preserved on the Severn Valley Railway. It is seen here near Ford and Crossgates en route to Kinnerley and Llanymynech. / *G. F. Bannister*

Above right: One of the earliest outings of preserved 2-6-2T No 4555, now on the Dart Valley Railway, was to Bromyard with a SLS special from Birmingham, Dudley and Stourbridge on 13 June 1964. The train is seen nearing Bromyard. / *M. Mensing*

Right: On 22 June 1963, the SLS ran a railtour which roamed the Birmingham and Wolverhampton area for seven hours behind a LNW Super D. The train is seen here at Oxley after travelling from Dudley and Wolverhampton Low Level. / *Harold D. Bowtell*

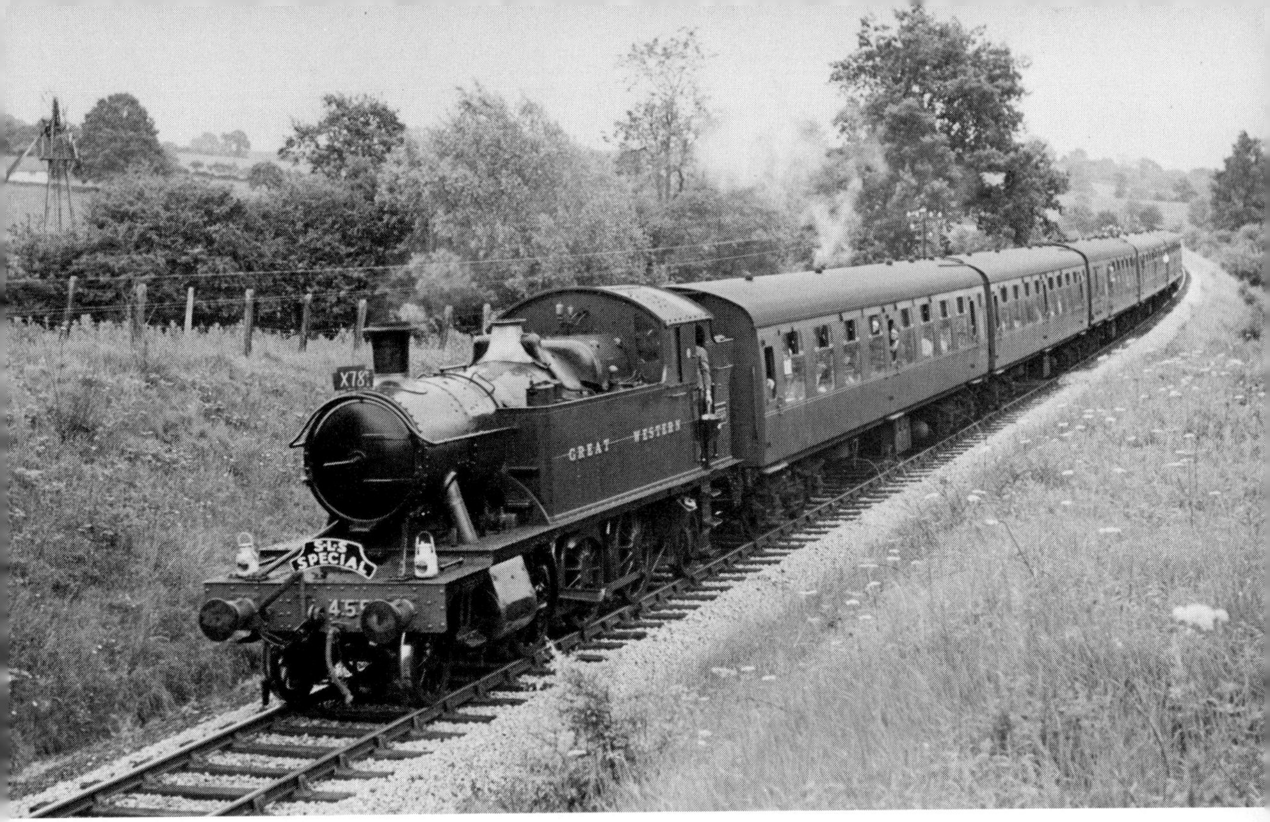
SLS
SPECIAL
GREAT WESTERN

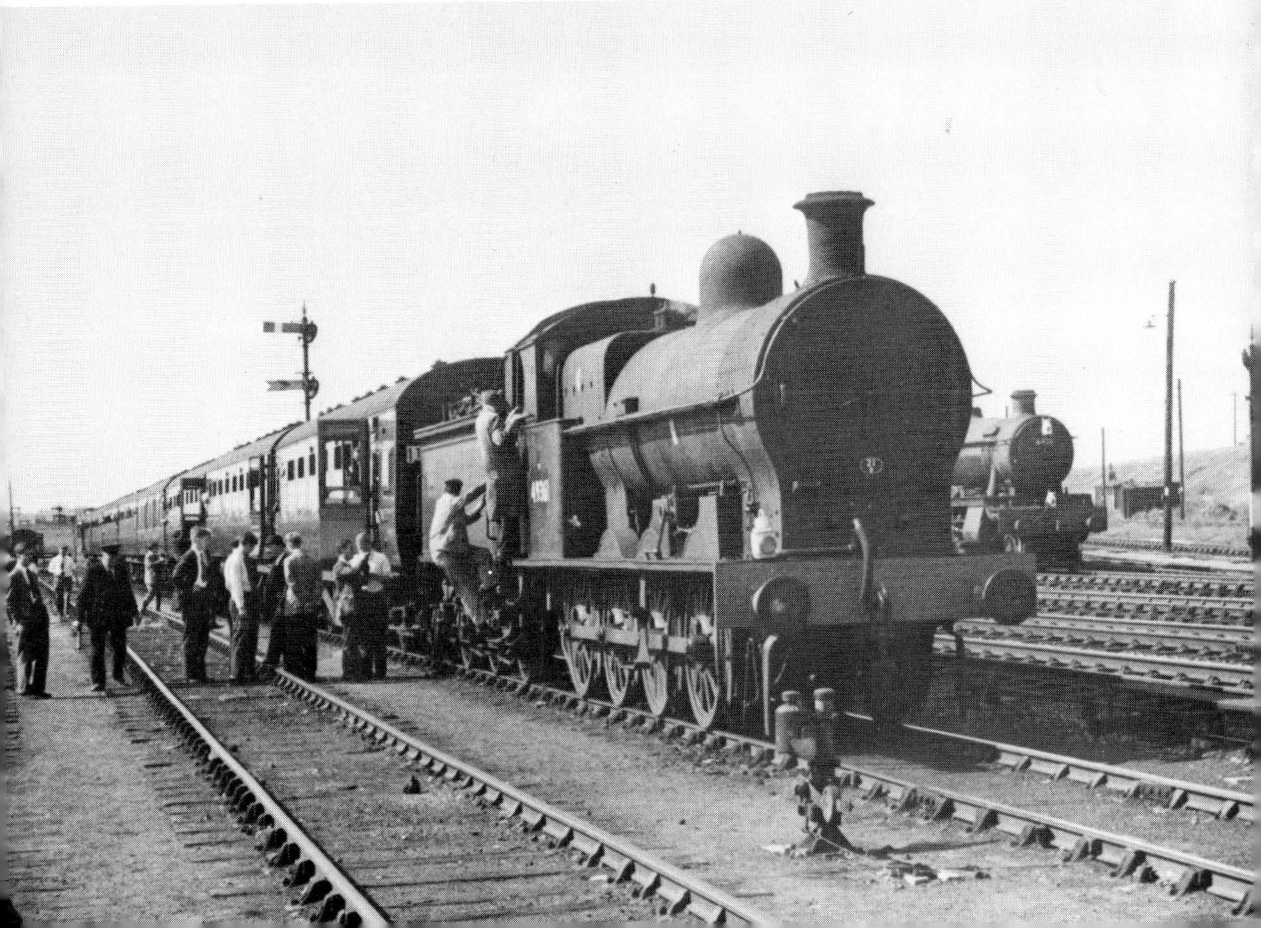

Above: In November 1962 the National Model Railroad Association hired Collett 0-6-0 No 2210 for a day so that members could drive a full size engine. The Association models American prototypes — hence the bell and white flags. / *R. E. James-Robertson*

Below: Since steam ended on British Rail, two lines in the West Midlands have been passed for steam running. The Great Western Society ran their splendidly restored GW set of coaches to Hereford via Worcester and Malvern on 14 June 1975 behind No 7808 *Cookham Manor* and No 6998 *Burton Agnes Hall*. They are seen here approaching Evesham on the return journey. Sadly this route is no longer available, so steam specials are confined to the Tyseley to Didcot & Stratford lines. / *Andrew D. Bannister*

Industrials

Below: Cannock and Rugeley Collieries 0-6-0ST No 1 *Marquis*, built in 1867 at the Lillieshall Company's works, in a classic rural coalfield setting at Rawnsley on Cannock Chase in 1957. */ G. F. Bannister*

Bottom: Hudswell Clark 0-6-0ST *The Colonel*, built in 1914, stands outside Grove Colliery shed, Brownhills on 30 April 1957. */ G. F. Bannister*

Above: On the fringe of Cannock Chase, Manning Wardle 0-6-0ST *Littleton No 5* of 1922 heads a load of empty wagons from the BR exchange sidings at Penkridge to Littleton Colliery, Huntington in April 1971. The engine is about to cross the Stafford and Worcester Canal and pass under the M6 motorway. / *G. F. Bannister*

Top right: The afternoon 'Paddy' between Rawnsley and Hednesford on the former Cannock & Rugeley Colliery Co line c1953. The engine is 0-6-0T No 8 *Harrison*, built by the Yorkshire Engine Co in 1872. / *P. B. Whitehouse*

Right: Also on the Cannock & Rugeley Colliery Co line, 0-6-0ST No 3 *Progress* built by Peckett in 1899 hard at work on a train of empties nearer Hednesford c1953. / *P. B. Whitehouse*

Preservation

Above: The Severn Valley Railway was closed to passengers between Bewdley and Shrewsbury in September 1963. On 23 May 1970, the Bridgnorth to Hampton Loade section reopened under the auspices of a preservation society and limited company. Since then the line has been reopened to Bewdley and it is intended to link up with British Rail at Kidderminster in the future. LMS 8F 2-8-0 No 8233 enters Highley en route to Bewdley on 14 May 1977. This engine is owned by the Stanier 8F Locomotive Society and has seen service in Persia and Egypt. / *Anthony J. Lambert*

Above right: GW 2-6-2T No 4566 was rescued from Barry scrapyard in 1970 and authentically restored to her state when new. She is seen here entering Highley station with a rake of Great Western coaches on the SVR Gala Day on 10 April 1976. / *Anthony J. Lambert*

Right: Gala Days on the SVR see the running of steam-hauled goods trains for the benefit of photographers — an appreciated opportunity to see a naturally uncommon sight. Pannier tank No 5764 leaves the picturesque station at Arley for Bridgnorth on 10 April 1976. / *Anthony J. Lambert*

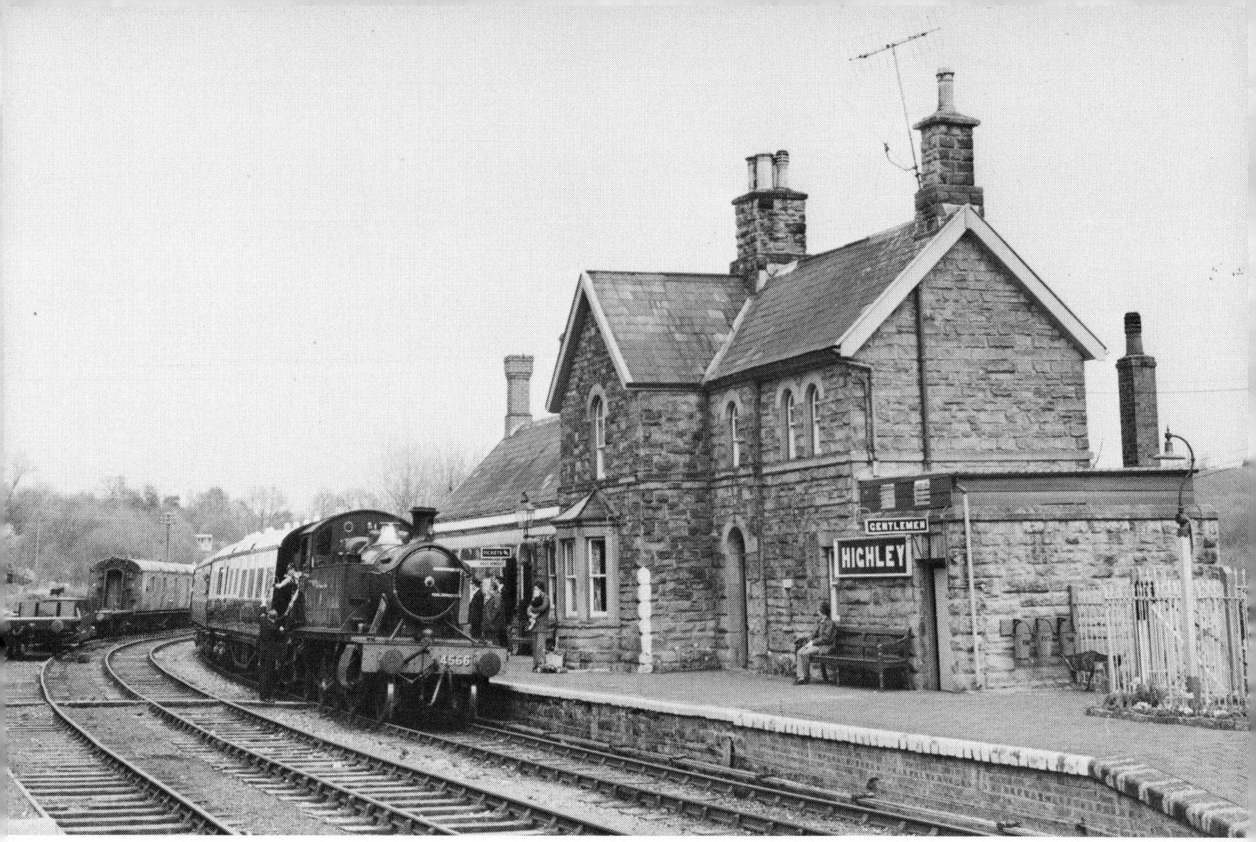
GENTLEMEN
HIGHLEY
4566

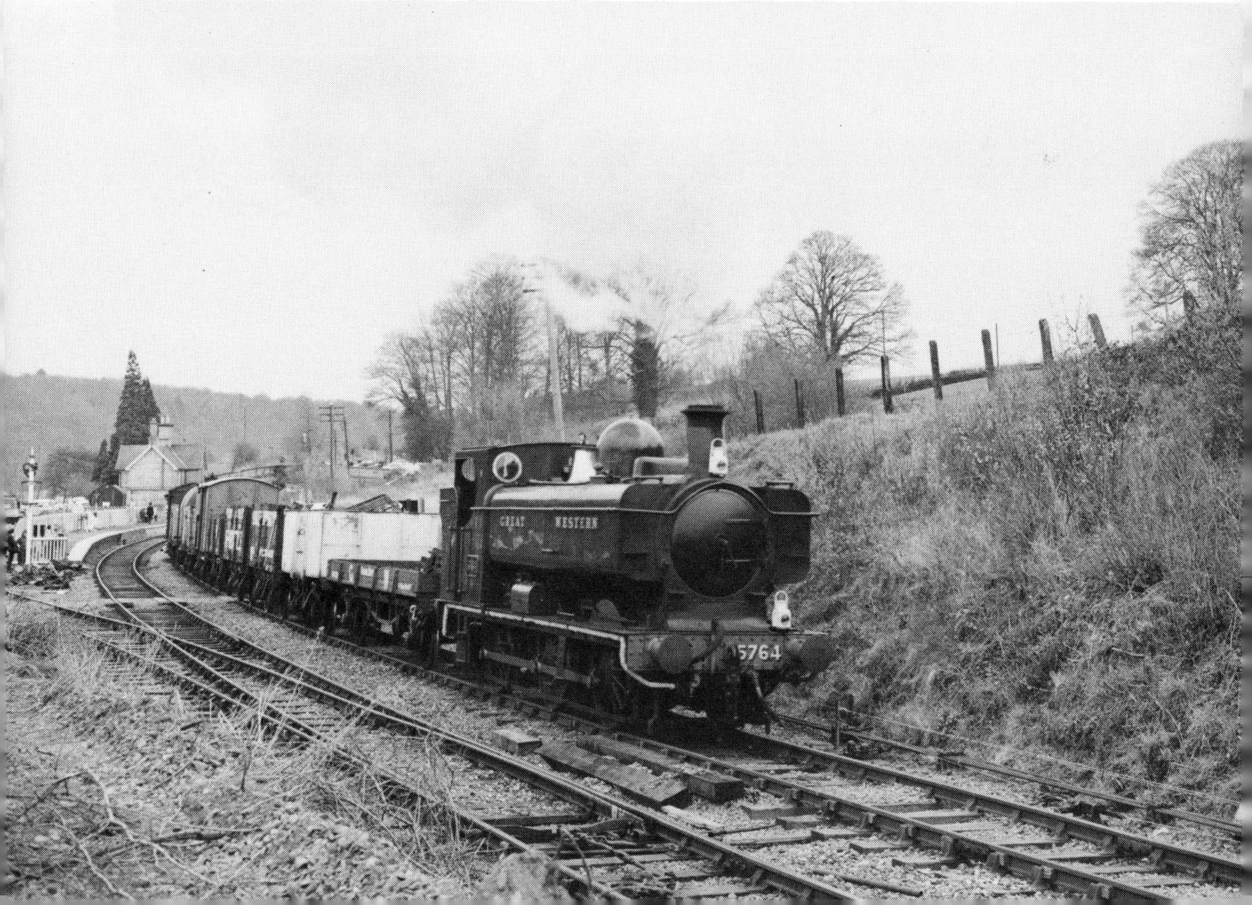
GREAT WESTERN
5764

Above: Ivatt 2-6-0 No 46443 was purchased in 1967 from British Railways and was an early arrival on the SVR. No 46443 was 'doctored' to appear in the film *Seven Per Cent Solution* as a Ruritanian concontion. Alongside is Manning Wardle 0-6-0ST No 2047 of 1926. *Warwickshire* was the last engine to be built by the Leeds firm which went into voluntary liquidation in 1927. They are seen here at Bridgnorth on 14 May 1977.
/ *Anthony J. Lambert*

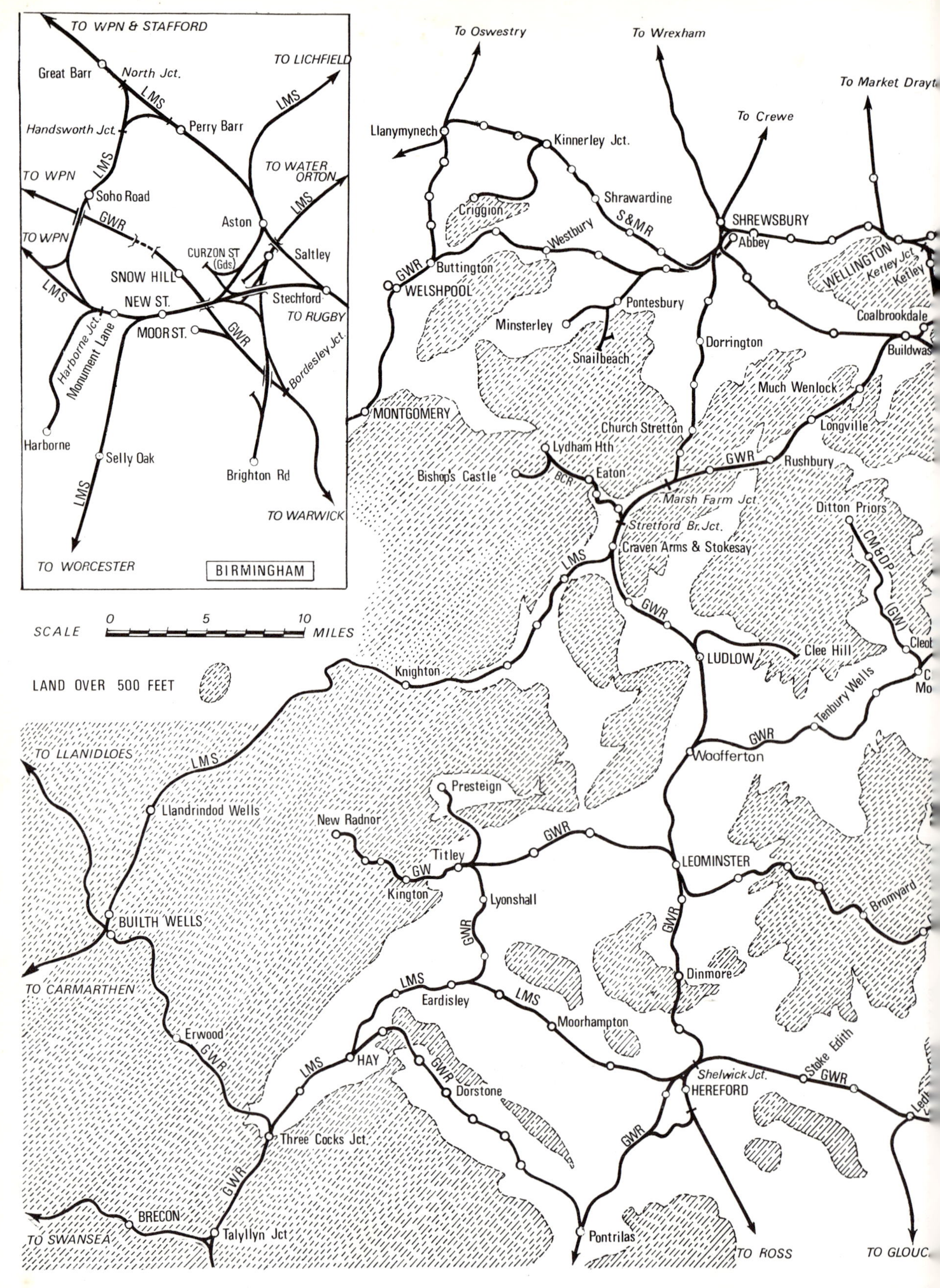

TO WPN & STAFFORD
TO LICHFIELD
Great Barr
North Jct.
LMS
LMS
Handsworth Jct.
Perry Barr
TO WATER ORTON
TO WPN
LMS
Soho Road
GWR
Aston
LMS
TO WPN
CURZON ST (Gds)
Saltley
SNOW HILL
NEW ST.
Stechford
TO RUGBY
LMS
Harborne Jct.
Monument Lane
MOOR ST.
GWR
Bordesley Jct.
Harborne
Selly Oak
Brighton Rd
LMS
TO WARWICK
TO WORCESTER
BIRMINGHAM
SCALE
0   5   10
MILES
LAND OVER 500 FEET
To Oswestry
To Wrexham
To Market Drayt
To Crewe
Llanymynech
Kinnerley Jct.
Shrawardine
SHREWSBURY
Criggion
S&MR
Abbey
WELLINGTON
Ketley Jct.
Ketley
GWR
Buttington
Westbury
WELSHPOOL
Coalbrookdale
Pontesbury
Minsterley
Dorrington
Buildwas
Snailbeach
Much Wenlock
MONTGOMERY
Church Stretton
Longville
Lydham Hth
GWR
Rushbury
Bishop's Castle
BCR
Eaton
Marsh Farm Jct.
Ditton Priors
Stretford Br. Jct.
CM&DP
(GW)
LMS
Craven Arms & Stokesay
GWR
Clee Hill
Cleot
LUDLOW
C
Mo
Knighton
Tenbury Wells
GWR
Woofferton
TO LLANIDLOES
LMS
Presteign
Llandrindod Wells
New Radnor
GWR
Titley
LEOMINSTER
GW
Bromyard
Kington
Lyonshall
BUILTH WELLS
GWR
Dinmore
LMS
TO CARMARTHEN
Eardisley
LMS
Erwood
Moorhampton
Stoke Edith
GWR
LMS
HAY
Shelwick Jct.
GWR
GWR
Dorstone
HEREFORD
Led
Three Cocks Jct.
GWR
BRECON
GWR
Talyllyn Jct.
Pontrilas
TO SWANSEA
TO ROSS
TO GLOUC